GLORY DAYS

Metropolitan Railway

John Glover

Ian Allan
PUBLISHING

The 1904 coat of arms of the Metropolitan Railway is displayed on the former Chesham branch coach at the LT Museum. The arms signify (from top left, clockwise) the arms of the City of London, and the counties of Middlesex, Hertfordshire and Buckinghamshire. The fist and the flashes represent electrical energy. *John Glover*

CONTENTS

First published 1998

ISBN 0 7110 2630 0

Published by Ian Allan Publishing

an imprint of Ian Allan Publishing Ltd, Terminal House, Station Approach, Shepperton, Surrey TW17 8AS.
Printed by Ian Allan Printing Ltd, Riverdene Business Park, Hersham, Surrey KT12 4RG.

Code: 9809/B3

INTRODUCTION

The former Metropolitan Railway is an essential component of the capital's railway system. In today's terms it covers the line out to Amersham and its various branches, the Hammersmith & City – and 'City' really means Barking, the Circle and the East London Line. The Metropolitan was not always the owner of these lines, but if it did not own them it was able to exercise running rights. Another Metropolitan appendage was the Great Northern & City line between Finsbury Park and Moorgate, now owned by Railtrack and operated by West Anglia Great Northern Railway.

This book sets out the main elements which brought the Metropolitan into being and the ways in which the company's development was shaped. The results were often less than conventional!

After a lifetime as an independent company, the Metropolitan was, against its wishes, absorbed into the newly created London Passenger Transport Board in 1933. Did this turn out to be to the passengers' advantage or not? An examination of the Metropolitan as it is today follows,

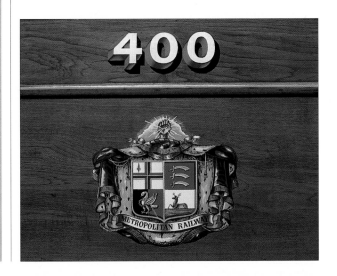

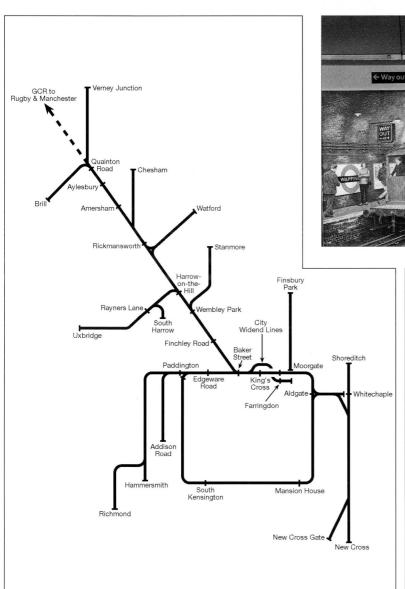

The Metropolitan Railway diagram shows the following stations:

GCR to Rugby & Manchester, Verney Junction, Quainton Road, Chesham, Aylesbury, Brill, Amersham, Watford, Rickmansworth, Stanmore, Harrow-on-the-Hill, Finsbury Park, Rayners Lane, Wembley Park, South Harrow, Uxbridge, City Widend Lines, Finchley Road, Baker Street, Paddington, Moorgate, Shoreditch, Edgeware Road, King's Cross, Aldgate, Whitechaple, Farringdon, Addison Road, Hammersmith, South Kensington, Mansion House, Richmond, New Cross Gate, New Cross

WAPPING

← Way out

and the network development plans which might affect it. The motive power and the change from steam to electric traction is also discussed.

The Metropolitan made a distinct contribution to the development of London and particularly the lands to the northwest and into Buckinghamshire. Without that company's enterprising approach, the suburban developments might have taken a very different form. The company's metals extended eventually over 50 miles from the nearest point on the Circle Line, which was quite an achievement for a concern whose original line was under four miles in length.

John Glover
Worcester Park, Surrey
August 1998

◄ **Wapping station walls now have a series of murals, including this one of times past and showing an F stock train and a BR goods. Where else can one now see a 20-ton brake van?**
John Glover

◄ **The Metropolitan Railway, showing services operated from time to time on a regular basis.**

1. A GROWING RAILWAY

Stanmore has a model interchange, with buses terminating immediately outside the station building. The architecture is very much the standard fare for the era; the station was opened on 10 December 1932. *John Glover*

To give the signal to start a train, the Metropolitan used this metal device to short circuit the two wires and sound a bell within the driver's hearing. This got over the problems of restricted visibility on curved platforms and the use of multiple-unit type bell signals with steam locomotive-hauled trains. The photograph is dated 17 September 1932. Such methods survived until the early 1960s. *Modern Transport*

The ubiquitous 4-4-0Ts built by Beyer Peacock of Gorton in 1864 are shown in this drawing, with condensing gear and also a full cab. Cabs were added from 1905, since electrification had displaced those locomotives remaining in stock to a generally open-air environment. *Courtesy Ian Beattie,* Railway Modeller *magazine*

Large concerns often start from small beginnings. The original 3.75-mile route of what became the Metropolitan Railway between Paddington and Farringdon was financed principally by the Corporation of the City of London and the Great Western Railway. The first was interested in alleviating traffic congestion; some things never change! The City's concern was the speed of movement of goods on the streets, which was a result of large numbers of slow-moving horse-drawn vehicles. The GWR, on the other hand, was interested in getting intended passengers to Paddington as well as establishing a through rail route to the City.

The whole concept of the urban underground railway, clear as it may be today, was less than obvious in those early days. The result, after many false starts, was the genesis of the Metropolitan Railway and, eventually, of London Underground as a whole. Charles Pearson, City solicitor, had the imagination to see what could be achieved, and pursued his ideas tenaciously. Pearson, for instance, was credited as early as 1858 with the view that 'the provision of cheap railway accommodation (would) enable the working classes to reside in the adjacent country districts'.

The *Illustrated London News* published this description of the works in 1860, still nearly three years from the Metropolitan's eventual opening on 10 January 1863:

This remarkable undertaking – which has been so long in abeyance that the public had well nigh despaired of its ultimate accomplishment – has now been

Scale: 4mm - 1ft

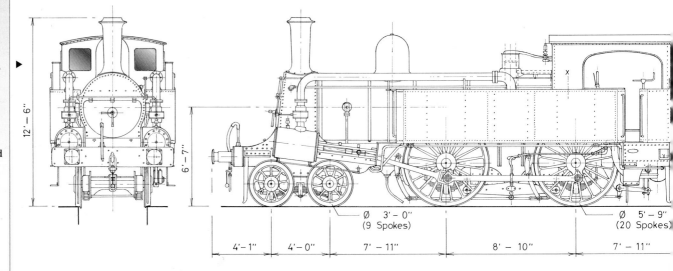

commenced in earnest, and the contractors are proceeding vigorously with the work at various points.

It is intended to run light trains at short intervals, and calling perhaps at alternate stations, and all risk of collision will be avoided by telegraphing the arrival and departure of each train from station to station, so that there will always be an interval of at least one station between the trains. The traffic is to be worked by locomotive engines of a novel and ingenious construction. In order to obviate the annoyance in a tunnel arising from smoke and the products of combustion, the locomotives will have no firebox, but will be charged with hot water and steam at a certain pressure to be supplied by fixed boilers at the termini, and will be furnished with a large heater to assist in maintaining the temperature. It is estimated that each locomotive will thus carry with it sufficient power to enable it to effect the double journey.

Well, technical specifications change, but the above perhaps indicates some of the obstacles to be overcome in what was an entirely new venture. The contractors had to drive their way through a network of water mains, gas mains and sewers, while ensuring that the adjacent buildings did not collapse into the 'cut and cover' railway construction. Despite the bursting of the Fleet Ditch sewer in June 1862, which filled the workings with 10ft of 'water' for a considerable distance, this was the only check to construction.

Completed it was, and the line was an immediate success. Over 29,000 passengers used it daily over the first three weeks. From the beginning, the passenger services on the mixed gauge line were worked by the Great Western, with its own locomotives and rolling stock. The standard gauge track was for access by the Great Northern for freight purposes, through a connection beneath King's Cross.

Smouldering disagreements between the Metropolitan and the Great Western soon came to a head. Precipitately, the GW withdrew its trains on 10 August 1863. The company had previously given notice on 18 July that it

Leaf fall timetable

UNDERGROUND Chorleywood

Tube Guide

Including new times from 24 September 1995

▲ Cover of the leaf fall edition tube guide for Chorleywood station, autumn 1995. (What tube?) It shows a present-day 55 Broadway view of Metro-land.

The generous dimensions of the original Metropolitan Railway route accommodated the GWR's broad gauge as well as standard gauge. The extension of the platform width into the tunnel area is especially noticeable. This view shows an A stock train departing from Great Portland Street towards Baker Street on 22 April 1998. *John Glover* ▶

◀◀ Compartment stock can be constructed to very tight dimensions; the seats in the Chesham coach are decidedly upright. The Metropolitan's customary round-topped doors may also be seen. *John Glover*

◀ Willesden Green was one of the many Metropolitan stations reconstructed around the time of World War 1; the entrance here proudly displays its origins, albeit that the station has been served first by the Bakerloo and then by the Jubilee lines for nearly 60 years. This picture was taken on 28 December 1996. *John Glover*

would cease to work the railway from 1 October. Interestingly, one of the causes of friction was the Metropolitan's wish to provide more than a 15min frequency service; the Great Western feared that this would merely increase costs disproportionately to revenue. In matters such as this, Underground companies have never agreed fully with their main line railway counterparts.

It may be noted here that the Metropolitan was the first railway to be worked throughout by absolute block signalling, with all points and signals interlocked. The capacity to operate safely at high frequencies was thus built into the design of the infrastructure.

The Metropolitan turned, successfully, to the Great Northern for help, and this was forthcoming. The Metropolitan was yet to own its own locomotives and coaching stock.

After the first year's working, the Metropolitan was shown to possess the most concentrated traffic of any railway then in existence:

Passenger receipts per route mile per week, 1864

	miles	£
Metropolitan	3.75	720.80
London, Chatham & Dover	84	79.66
South Eastern	306	53.42
London, Brighton & South Coast	268	53.20
London & North Western	1,274	41.15
Great Northern	404	34.39
London & South Western	490	34.20
London, Tilbury & Southend	42	28.48
Great Western	1,269	27.98
Midland	663	22.19
Great Eastern	673	22.16

It might be added that the main line railways also derive substantial revenues from freight which, at this stage, was not the case with the Metropolitan. The Metropolitan's infrastructure costs would also have been high, but nevertheless this still represents a remarkable performance.

This success soon had the railway extended, both within and then outside the then built up area. Over the ensuing 20 years or so, the Metropolitan Railway expanded as follows:

1863	Paddington-Farringdon
1864	Paddington-Hammersmith/Kensington Addison Road
1865	Farringdon-Moorgate
1868	Widened Lines King's Cross-Moorgate completed
1868	Baker Street-Swiss Cottage (Met)
1868	Edgware Road-South Kensington
1875	Moorgate-Liverpool Street
1876	Liverpool Street-Aldgate
1879	Swiss Cottage (Met)-Willesden Green (Met)
1880	Willesden Green-Harrow-on-the-Hill
1882	Aldgate-Tower Hill
1884	Liverpool Street-Whitechapel
1884	Tower Hill-Mansion House, jointly with District
1884	East London Railway running rights leased to six companies, including the Metropolitan

A number of forces were at work. The westwards extension to Hammersmith was built by a separate company, which had the support of the Great Western as well as the Metropolitan. Worked initially by the GWR, the line became a joint responsibility of both companies when friendly relations were re-established. Like the original section of the Metropolitan, this was constructed with mixed gauge track.

The branch to Addison Road – Kensington Olympia in present-day terms – has long since disappeared, but it allowed access to the West London Line and all that this implied in terms of choice of destinations. There was also a connection to the London & South Western Railway at Hammersmith, again over a long-abandoned connection via what became today's District Line service to Richmond.

Other extensions, to some extent in collaboration with the Metropolitan District company, set about the eventual creation of the Circle Line. This was a prime objective of Parliament, although its completion had to wait until 1884.

Of more import to the Metropolitan was the building of the Widened Lines. These quadrupled the original route east of King's Cross through to Moorgate, for the benefit primarily of freight from the GNR. This construction entailed the doubling of the Clerkenwell tunnels and a dive-under between King's Cross and Farringdon (the Ray Street Gridiron) to move the Widened Lines from the north to the south side of the Metropolitan without obstructing traffic flows on the latter. It was on the south side that the City goods depots were located, and the Widened Lines also formed a jumping-off point to the London Chatham & Dover Railway at Blackfriars.

The Widened Lines also provided the Midland Railway with access to Moorgate for passenger services, and they were thus used by the other railways as well. In this part of Moorgate station, the number of platforms expanded eventually to eight. Of these, six remain today.

In late Victorian times, direct access to and from the Metropolitan's core network was enjoyed by as many as six main line railway companies, but the attractiveness diminished with the growth of the tube network and the rise of the bus.

There were also the first signs of the expansion to the northwest, with the opening of the branch to Swiss Cottage (1.8 miles from Baker Street) extended in a short time to Willesden Green (4.0 miles) and then to Harrow-on-the-Hill (9.3 miles). The purpose was the pursuit of what was seen as potentially profitable suburban traffic. As much of the territory was in green fields, today's stations often came later. This was in the same general direction as the areas served already by the London & North Western Railway from Euston, and via its North London Railway associate to and from the City at Broad Street.

The East London Line has a remarkable past, since it came into being as a result of Sir Mark Brunel's pioneering work on the building of a bored tunnel between Wapping and Rotherhithe. This was completed after many vicissitudes in 1843. Constructed for horse-drawn vehicles, the access ramps could never be afforded, and its initial use was for pedestrians only.

In 1869, Brunel's twin tunnels were adapted for railway use and extended progressively as the East London Railway. Various companies provided services. These included both

▲ The Verney Junction outpost is nowadays a little sad. The station house still stands, as do the remains of the two island platforms. This view is taken on 10 April 1998, looking west towards Oxford; the single-track line is mothballed out of use. The platform used formerly by the Metropolitan was that on the left side of the island and next to the house. *John Glover*

◄◄ The Chiltern Court flats were intended by the Metropolitan to be a hotel above Baker Street station, but flats were substituted during construction in the 1920s. Ground level includes the ticket office and some shops. *John Glover*

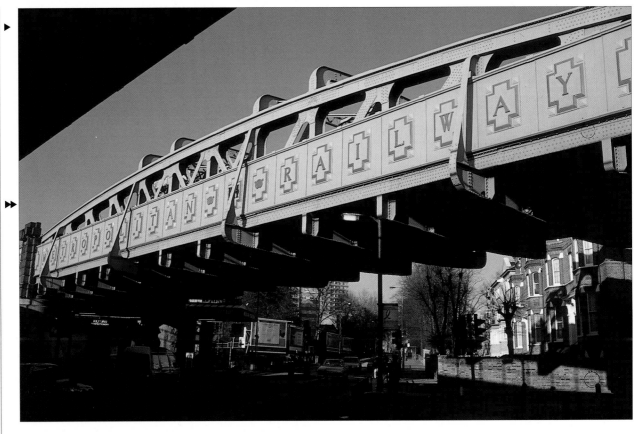

This is the street-level view of a complex crossing of a series of roads by six tracks of railway at a station serving a total of four platforms. This bridge carries the southbound Metropolitan and Jubilee lines. The location is Kilburn, looking north up the A5, on 28 December 1996. *John Glover*

The Hammersmith & City Line crosses the GW main line out of Paddington between Royal Oak and Westbourne Park. Originally, this was a flat crossing, but the position soon became untenable and a replacement subway was constructed. An eastbound C stock train for Barking descends to the tunnel in July 1989 as a train for Hammersmith approaches. *John Glover*

the Metropolitan and District Railways from 1884, but these services were withdrawn in 1906 and 1905 respectively. The line was electrified in 1913, from which time the passenger services were operated by the Metropolitan on a permanent basis. Today, there are nine stations, including the yet to be opened Canada Water.

The next 20-year period saw the Metropolitan Railway reach almost its greatest extent with these lines commissioned:

1885   Harrow-on-the-Hill-Pinner
1887   Pinner-Rickmansworth

1889   Rickmansworth-Chalfont & Latimer-Chesham
1891   Aylesbury-Verney Junction (acquired by Metropolitan Rly; opened 1868)
1892   Chalfont & Latimer-Amersham-Aylesbury
1899   Quainton Road-Brill (worked by Metropolitan Rly; opened 1871)
1904   Harrow-on-the-Hill-Uxbridge

The push to the Chilterns was continuous, and due in no small part to the influence and ambitions of Sir Edward Watkin. A Manchester man, he became Chairman of the

Metropolitan in 1872, a position he held until 1894.

Watkin had, be it said, many other business interests. These included the Manchester, Sheffield & Lincolnshire Railway (later the Great Central), the East London Railway, the South Eastern Railway and the Channel Tunnel Co. It was undoubtedly due to his energy and ambition that the Metropolitan pursued its northern drive. It is said that he had a vision of a railway from Manchester to Paris, run by companies largely under his control or, at least, in which he would have a strong influence.

Thus the expansion of the Metropolitan was a means of breaking through the existing railway networks around London, with a line to be linked eventually with the Manchester, Sheffield & Lincolnshire in that company's bid for access to the south. But the suburbanisation of what became known as Metro-land was a worthwhile business in itself.

Like many, if not most, railway companies, the Metropolitan often acquired more land for railway building than was strictly needed. One immediate aim was to make sure that the company had the land specified in its 'limits of deviation', which its authorising Act gave it to meet unforeseen difficulties in construction without needing to seek further enabling legislation. The other was to satisfy landowners who refused to sell the land required for the railway without adding on a great deal more adjoining land from their holdings.

The Metropolitan bought all of it, but far from selling it off again as was generally required by Parliament, the Metropolitan managed to manipulate its own Acts to help it profit from its land holdings. These culminated in 1873 with a provision which enabled the company to retain any surplus lands, whenever acquired, including those to be acquired in the future. Through this, and subsequent legislation, the Metropolitan manoeuvred itself into a position whereby it was able to develop land for residential purposes. This was through the aegis of its Surplus Lands Committee.

Beyond Rickmansworth, the most obvious destination was Chesham, this being the only town of any consequence in the area. And so it turned out to be, with the

Metropolitan reaching it in 1889. A gift by the townspeople of £2,000 ensured that land would be purchased for a centrally placed station rather than it being stuck on the outskirts. For an example of a practical gift of lasting benefit to the town as well as the company, this was hard to beat.

But the line was constructed as a single track branch beyond Chalfont, and it became clear that Aylesbury would be the next target for the expanding company. The county town was reached in 1892 by the Metropolitan, but in a sense the company was already there. For the Aylesbury & Buckingham Railway had built itself a line from Verney Junction to Quainton Road and Aylesbury.

Verney Junction was on the Oxford-Cambridge line, a settlement which even today boasts no more than a dozen houses. As this line headed in the general direction which the Metropolitan was seeking to follow, the company purchased the Aylesbury & Buckingham in 1891. This was a year before the Metropolitan's own line from the south was ready for traffic. The new owners doubled the single track line, with the work completed in 1897. Quite why a four trains per day service should have justified this is unclear.

The most remarkable or, according to one's point of view, ridiculous involvement of the Metropolitan was its agreement to work the Duke of Buckingham's private railway from Quainton Road to Brill. The primary purpose of this line was to carry supplies and produce in connection with the Duke's own estates. The line was 6.5 miles long. Not many people have enough land and capital to consider building a personally owned private railway, even if tramway was probably a more accurate description.

The public were carried as passengers, though not initially. By 1899, four trains per day were operated, most with a journey time of 40min or less than 10mph average speed. Passengers leaving Brill on the 8.10am departure could arrive at Baker Street at 11.08, though if they preferred Paddington or Euston, arrival in either case was not until 12.40pm.

The Metropolitan's interest was the potential for an extension of the tramway to Oxford, but this came to nothing.

The third railway at Quainton Road approached from the north, where the Great Central (GC) arrived in 1898. From here, running powers were granted by the Metropolitan to a point immediately south of Harrow-on-the-Hill, and then over two new tracks which the Metropolitan constructed on the south side of its own through to a point just short of Finchley Road at Canfield Place. From here the Great Central constructed its own tunnelled approach to its Marylebone terminus, which was opened in 1899.

The interdependence of these arrangements led to the formation of the Met and GC Joint Committee, to which the Metropolitan leased the existing line from Verney Junction through to Harrow. The newly constructed line southwards was leased to the Great Central.

It may be noted here that a condition which the Metropolitan imposed on the GC to protect its own traffic was that there should be no station south of Harrow-on-the-Hill. By such methods was the railway system shaped in the late Victorian era.

On a less exotic note, a little nearer London the company looked west, to the long-established market town of Uxbridge. A six-mile branch was constructed from Harrow-on-the-Hill and opened in 1904, but traffic generation was slow. The line was opened with steam traction. Electrification though was now in the offing, and followed shortly afterwards on 1 January 1905. A running connection from South Harrow to Rayners Lane, now used by the Piccadilly but then by the District, followed six years later.

In the 30 years which were left until the company was absorbed by the London Passenger Transport Board, route developments were fewer.

The Great Northern & City Railway (GN&CR) had opened its tube line from Finsbury Park to Moorgate in 1904, and this undertaking was acquired by the Metropolitan in 1913. It was perhaps the sort of railway that the Metropolitan could appreciate, since it was built to a similar loading gauge.

The GN&CR was also an early user of electric multiple-units, and the workshops and depot were alongside the station at Drayton Park. The company had built its own power station at Poole Street, midway between Old Street and Essex Road stations. The traction current reached the trains through two conductor rails, each placed outside the running rails.

The Metropolitan, it seems, felt that acquisition would protect its own interests and allow some developments, but in reality the company did little more than introduce First Class travel in 1915 and substitute its own electric power supply, generated at Neasden.

Mention has already been made of the company's housing interests, but a larger scale business was now envisaged by Robert Selbie, the then General Manager. The concept was to be sold as Metro-land. A new company, Metropolitan Railway Country Estates Ltd, would be set up, and in this the railway would have a controlling interest. Formed in 1919, this company was to develop land already owned by the railway, as well as other land purchases made for the purpose.

The net result was that the Metropolitan engineered itself into a position whereby the railway provided the

track, stations and the train services, and then ensured that the land was available for housebuilding. The estates would be laid out, the housing designed and the erection of houses supervised. The new occupants would then be highly likely to make daily use of the railway and hence ensure the Metropolitan's future revenues.

Such a scheme was unique in Britain, although elsewhere, as in the United States west of the Mississippi, land concessions were given to railroad investors to encourage the building of railways where traffic was non-existent. This does not quite fit the image of 'a rural outpost yet close to London' as Metro-land was described, but there are similarities to the American approach.

There had been many who, over the years, had been appalled by the squalor of urban Britain. It was not altogether unfair that London was known as 'the smoke'. Thus had begun a movement in the early part of the 20th century pioneering the self-contained Garden City concept, led by the vision and idealism of Ebenezer Howard who created Garden Cities around London, first at Letchworth and then at Welwyn. Later, this gave rise to the New Towns.

▲ The limited width of many of the platforms on the East London Line is noticeable in this picture of Shadwell, looking south on 18 April 1998. A Whitechapel train approaches, crossing a southbound service.
John Glover

The aim of the Metropolitan Railway was different, however, since the creation of the need to travel was an end in itself. The Metropolitan's activities, like those of many speculative builders, led to the construction of rows of mock-Tudor houses. The difference was that the Metropolitan ensured that all the construction in which it was involved was carried out in sites which were ideally suited for travel to work in central London by its services. 'Metro-land' was conceived essentially as a commuter-based community for the reasonably, or in some cases decidedly, well-heeled.

Company literature of the 1920s indicates the sales pitch which was adopted. Thus, the 500-acre Cedars Estate 'is notable for its delightful situation and its abundance of

◄◄ The GN&CR terminal car sheds were at Drayton Park on the west side of the line, nearest the camera in this view of 22 April 1998. This site has now been cleared, and indeed the WAGN trains now take a completely different above ground route to Finsbury Park high level station. No 313036 is seen departing northwards. The line at higher level beyond the station is that from Finsbury Park to the North London Line at Canonbury. *John Glover*

◄ The stairs leading to the platform at Drayton Park are attractively finished in this 1904 station. *John Glover*

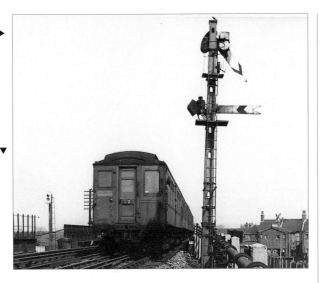

The District Line hand-worked door stock was used on the East London Line until 1953. A train of this stock is seen in this undated photograph with a New Cross Gate destination.
Author's collection

Rickmansworth became a changeover point to steam traction for passenger trains from 1925. It seems likely that this undated photograph was taken some time after that date and perhaps before the end of the Metropolitan Railway in 1933. *Author's collection*

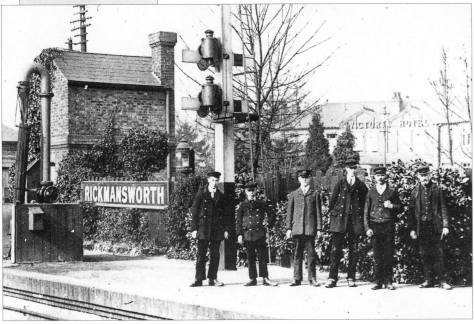

charming features and no more delectable spot could be desired as a place of residence. It is undulating in character; possesses a subsoil of gravel, sand and chalk; is conveniently situated near Rickmansworth station, and extends from this old-world country town westward over hill, dale and broad woodland to Chorley Wood's breezy common, where it is flanked by trim plantations that provide a perpetual feast for the eye.' To and from Rickmansworth and Chorley Wood (later to be spelled as one word), through trains ran at short intervals.

But, make no mistake, the Metro-land concept was popular. Championed and perhaps immortalised by the late Poet Laureate, Sir John Betjeman, a sojourn in the company's Baker Street buffet enabled him to conjure up a vision for all, in his poem *The Metropolitan Railway*. Where else in a public place could one enthuse over a stained glass windmill and a pot of tea, within a setting of fine woodwork and a smell of dinner? At the same time, it would seem that one could view sepia prints of Pinner's leafy lanes.

The net result was that the urbanisation of an area then known as northwest Middlesex was virtually complete by the outbreak of World War 2. The Metro-land idea extended into west Hertfordshire and to the south of Buckinghamshire, and was sustained by the Amersham electrification. Social engineering was unlikely to have been on the Metropolitan's agenda but the impact of the activities of Metropolitan Railway Country Estates Ltd will be felt for several generations.

Back on the Metropolitan main line, success was resulting in severe capacity problems. By the time World War 1 was under way, the line from Finchley Road to Wembley Park had been quadrupled. Extra platforms were built at Willesden Green, Neasden and Wembley Park stations only. Quadrupling was extended to Harrow-on-the-Hill by 1932.

Congestion in the Farringdon area led to some minor works and the eastbound-only electrification of the Widened Lines in 1926.

Another source of traffic was identified at Watford, and this was a joint venture with the London & North Eastern

Railway as successor to the Great Central. This line opened in 1925, together with the curve linking Watford to Rickmansworth. Services were provided to both Marylebone and Baker Street originally, but later to Baker Street only. To make this possible in a capacity sense, a burrowing junction was provided north of Harrow for Uxbridge branch trains.

And if Watford, why not Stanmore also? 1932 saw the opening of this 4.5-mile branch with the intermediate stations of Kingsbury and Canons Park and, in LPTB days,

Queensbury. Unlike Watford, which was already a sizeable community, the Stanmore branch was a speculative extension into a largely undeveloped area.

Whatever else these two new lines achieved, they did not contribute to the provision of more capacity south of Finchley Road. The reconstruction of Edgware Road station in 1926 to act as the start of a new tunnelled link to Kilburn saw no further progress. Resolution of that problem had to wait for the LPTB to solve, as we shall see.

The western side of the
Circle Line was built south
of Bayswater, as seen here,
in a cut. This was only
partially covered in. On
28 April 1997 a C stock
train approaches on a
Wimbledon-Edgware Road
service. *John Glover*

The sinuous curves at
Farringdon are seen as this
C stock Circle Line train
approaches from the King's
Cross direction. Passenger
loadings on both platforms
are substantial but it is
noticeable that most
passengers are keeping
behind the painted yellow
lines. The date is 22 April
1998. *John Glover*

2. FROM STEAM TO ELECTRIC TRACTION

The Metropolitan relied on steam traction from its opening; despite great concerns about the atmospheric conditions in the tunnels, it turned out that, effectively, there was then no other choice.

The company's first steam locomotive acquisitions from 1864 onwards were designed by Sir John Fowler, whose unsuccessful earlier fireless locomotive had been consigned to almost instant oblivion. These were the 'A' class Beyer Peacock 4-4-0Ts, with very prominent outside cylinders. These locomotives, originally 18 in number but by 1885 expanded to a fleet of 66 if the very similar 'B' class is included, were outstandingly successful. The exhaust from the cylinders was carried by large pipes to the side tanks, where the steam was condensed. Or at least this was the theory. In practice, condensation occurs only when the water into which the steam is fed is sufficiently cool, and this meant constant replacement. Time spent filling water tanks is not used productively for hauling trains. These locomotives remained at the helm of the inner area services until displaced by electrification in 1905-6. Some survived for many years, including at such outposts as Brill. No 23 may be found today in the LT Museum at Covent Garden.

In the author's view, the locomotives have a striking family resemblance to their contemporaries from the same builders, which today still work the 3ft-gauge Isle of Man steam railway.

They hauled gas-lit coaches from the Ashbury Railway Carriage and Iron Co, so the whole trains were the best Manchester products. Later batches of the carriages had what became a Metropolitan characteristic: the round-topped doors, which minimised the likelihood of their striking the tunnel walls if opened injudiciously. In a different world from that of today, three classes of travel were provided, and the Metropolitan was formally exempted from the Act of 1868 which required smoking accommodation to be provided on trains. However,

competitive pressures and public opinion resulted in both the Metropolitan and the Metropolitan District companies making provision from 1874.

Further steam locomotive construction at the turn of the century included the 'E' class 0-4-4Ts which reached seven in number (No 1 is preserved), and the four 'F' class 0-6-2Ts for freight work. As a result, the 'F' class was not fitted for steam heating.

More Ashbury bogie coaching stock was acquired from 1898 onwards for the longer distance services; these vehicles had a total length of a little over 42ft, making them decidedly short when compared with, say, the 53ft of today's A stock.

These compartment vehicles were formed into six-car sets and were fitted with dynamo-driven electric lighting. Later, with the spread of electrification, many of these vehicles were converted progressively to electric multiple-units and ran successfully to Uxbridge and then Stanmore. In this form, they lasted until World War 2. But vehicles were still required for the Chesham shuttle. Six of the 'bogie stock' vehicles were reconverted for steam push-pull operation as two three-car sets. When retired eventually in 1960, they were the oldest passenger coaches in use anywhere on the nationalised railway. Most of them have been preserved.

Further steam stock building was necessary for the ever growing railway. The 'Dreadnought' compartment coaches made their appearance in 1910 and the fleet was extended to 92 vehicles by 1923. These were very much standard main line steam-heated railway suburban coaches of their period; they were run on occasion with the two Pullman cars, *Mayflower* and *Galatea*, with which the Metropolitan tried to woo the people of Aylesbury and Chesham.

Even with the spread of electrification, steam power was still needed for passenger services on a diminishing but still very substantial section of line, and for all freight. This saw the construction of the following classes of tank engines:

Year	Class	Type	Builder	No	Main duties
1915	G	0-6-4T	Yorkshire Engine Co	4	passenger
1920	H	4-4-4T	Kerr, Stuart & Co	8	express passenger
1925	K	2-6-4T	Armstrong Whitworth	6	freight

Electrification

The tube railways showed from 1890 onwards that electricity was the traction of the future. In 1908, the Metropolitan carried out an experimental electrification, in conjunction with the Metropolitan District Railway, between Earl's Court and High Street Kensington. Given the interlocking of the two companies' services, it was important that the same technical standards were used, though deciding which was a cause of disagreement at the time. Dual-system equipment, which might be thought of as making the best of a bad job, was not then an option.

The Metropolitan opened its Neasden power station in 1905, and by 1908 electrification was completed on all the inner area services and on the main line to both Harrow-on-the-Hill and Uxbridge. This had the result of banishing steam workings on revenue-earning work south of Harrow,

The eight 4-4-4Ts were examples of what was an extremely unusual wheel arrangement, in Britain anyway. Intended for express passenger work, these handsome beasts were built by Kerr Stuart to the design of Charles Jones, the Metropolitan CME, in 1921-2.
Drawing by R. W. Rush, Model Railway Constructor

Scale 3mm - 1ft

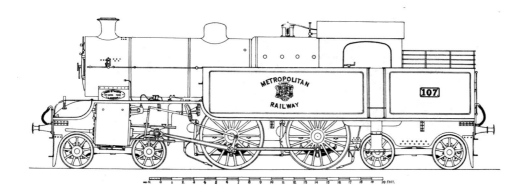

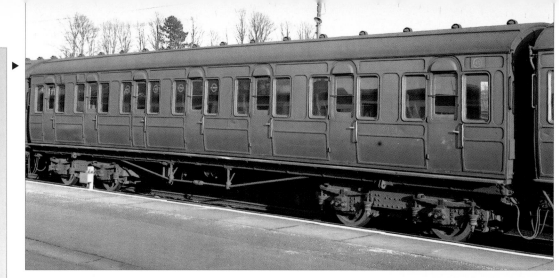

The T stock provided for more than one class of travel; this is car No 9721 at Watford on 24 March 1962. This vehicle has a seven-compartment layout, having formerly been First Class.
L. Sandler

This picture represents what might be termed the definitive view of the preserved Class A 4-4-0T locomotive No 23, outside the old power station at Neasden in January 1961. Did the Metropolitan *really* paint its steam locomotives, which were to spend most of their days underground, in such brilliant colours?
The late J. P. Mullett/Colour-Rail (LT27)

apart from freight to Finchley Road and for depot access to Neasden.

Early electric stock for the Metropolitan came from a number of sources. All were open saloon vehicles. The treatment of doors gave some problems; the original gate stock idea was decidedly passenger-unfriendly in the winter months on the extensive outdoor sections of line. Alternatives tried included sliding end doors and centre sliding double doors. All had their advantages and disadvantages in terms of loading and unloading speeds and hence the dwell time spent at stations, and the

seating capacity provided. A further complication was that the conditions on the Circle Line were rather different from the rural wastes which were found *en route* to Uxbridge.

Another oddity was the inclusion of a luggage compartment in some stock.

In 1906, Second Class accommodation was withdrawn, although First Class remained on some Metropolitan services into the LPTB era. Its provision was another potential cause of delay in boarding, since passengers needed to seek the right portion of their train.

◀ The Metropolitan developed the freight business, but it also generated some traffic of its own. In April 1957, Peckett 0-6-0T No L53 is seen shunting coal wagons brought to Neasden to feed the Metropolitan's huge power station which forms the background to this picture. The power station itself opened on 1 December 1904 and closed finally on 21 July 1968.
L. V. Reason/Colour-Rail (LT137)

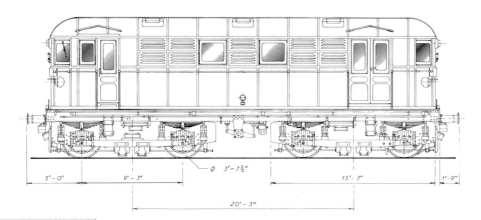

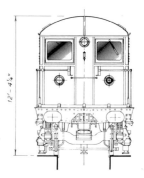

Scale: 3mm - 1ft

Where part of a journey was completed on electrified tracks, and some not, an engine change was required if steam operation was to be kept out of the in-town portions. The first 10 electric locomotives were built in 1904-6 by the Metropolitan Carriage & Wagon Co. These had the driving cab in the centre of the locomotive and sloping ends. The second 10 were built in 1907, with driving cabs at both ends and square fronts.

In 1922-3 all 20 were very extensively rebuilt by Metropolitan Vickers for higher performance, with new traction motors rated at 1,200hp. The locomotives were now able to reach 20mph in 25sec, attaining a maximum of 65mph on the level. Eight positive and four negative current-collector shoes were provided, but additional shoes on the brake vehicles of each train were connected by cable. Their purpose was to bridge gaps in the conductor rail at junctions. Braking was by vacuum or Westinghouse air.

Each locomotive was named. After the war, *Oliver Cromwell* became *Thomas Lord*, with cricketing rather than dictatorial connotations:

1 *John Lyon*	2 *Oliver Cromwell*
3 *Sir Ralph Verney*	4 *Lord Byron*
5 *John Hampden*	6 *William Penn*
7 *Edmund Burke*	8 *Sherlock Holmes*
9 *John Milton*	10 *William Ewart Gladstone*
11 *George Romney*	12 *Sarah Siddons*
13 *Dick Whittington*	14 *Benjamin Disraeli*
15 *Wembley 1924*	16 *Oliver Goldsmith*
17 *Florence Nightingale*	18 *Michael Faraday*
19 *John Wycliffe*	20 *Sir Christopher Wren*

Most lasted until the Amersham electrification, since which time No 12 has been maintained in usable condition. No 5 is in the LT Museum.

A further delivery of trains for the Circle Line commenced in 1921, to a total of 59 vehicles. The motor cars used the traction equipment removed from the earlier electric locomotives.

With the 1925 electrification north of Harrow and the opening of the Watford branch, there was a need for more electric rolling stock for the main line services. These compartment stock vehicles, which numbered eventually 182, were a mixture of new construction and conversions over a period from the 'Dreadnoughts'. They were delivered from 1927 onwards, and collectively they became known later as T stock.

Vehicles were a mixture of driving motors, trailers and

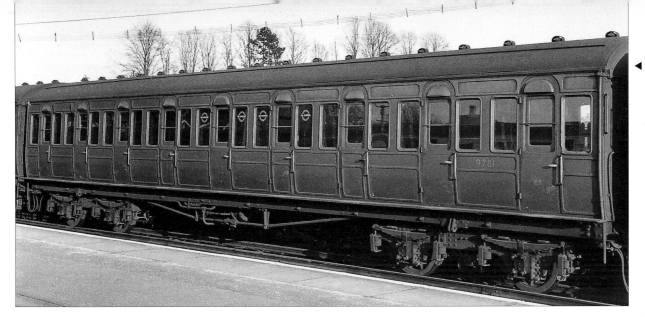

This T stock vehicle (No 9781), again photographed at Watford, was always Third Class, and as a result fitted nine compartments into a similar body length as car No 9721. This may be compared with the former 1st Class vehicle shown on p22. *L. Sandler*

The large 'K' class 2-6-4Ts of 1925 were impressive and powerful beasts. They were built from the 'kits' produced at Woolwich Arsenal from an SECR design. Erection was by Armstrong Whitworth, and the six locomotives were built as tank rather than tender locomotives. Doubtless the Metropolitan obtained them at a knock-down price, but they were too big to be used in the tunnels south of Finchley Road. However, freight work was their main purpose. *Ian Allan Library*

The Peckett No L53 is posed, gleaming in the sunshine, at Neasden in April 1957 (see p24). As the photographer comments, 'observe the parental pride!' The locomotive was originally Metropolitan Railway No 101 and was built in 1897. It was withdrawn in 1960, after a mere 63 years of service.
V. Reason/Colour-Rail (LT136)

From Surrey Docks (now Surrey Quays) the East London Line southwards is entirely in the open. A train of mixed Q stock, with Q27 Driving Motor No 4211 at the rear leaves for New Cross – or is it New Cross Gate? The older vehicles have clerestory roofs. It is August 1970.
Colour-Rail (LT8)

One of the original set of 10 Metropolitan electric locomotives from Westinghouse which dated from 1906. This shows a train with one of the Metropolitan's two Pullman cars leaving Harrow-on-the-Hill about 1910 behind Bo-Bo electric locomotive No 1.
Ian Allan Library/
A. B. Macleod collection

control trailers (ie cab but no motors). Latterly they were formed into trains of two motors plus four or six trailers, giving them a hefty 2,200hp worth of punch. There were many variations in this stock: early batches had wooden bodies, whereas later versions had steel-panelled bodies and were fitted with roller-bearing axleboxes.

Other electric units to be found on Metropolitan metals were the F stock cars built for the District in 1920-1. Later, these became surplus on the District due to the R stock deliveries. The F stock found its way to the Metropolitan's Uxbridge line trains from 1951, where their high acceleration rates made them most suitable for the speeds which could be maintained where stations are less closely spaced. Their three sets of double doors per vehicle side also gave them excellent crowd shifting capabilities. Visually, their elliptical cab front windows always made them immediately recognisable.

A last duty for these units was on the East London Line, reduced to four-car rather than eight-car formations. They were withdrawn finally in 1963.

For the in-town services, the Metropolitan relied latterly on the O and P stocks. The two types differed mainly in equipment provision and the positioning of guard's controls. Each vehicle was 51ft long, and car bodies

all had two sets of double and one set of single doors per side, plus a cab door. On the trailers, this curious arrangement was to ease their conversion subsequently to driving motors, which was effected in some cases. The O and P stock were built in the period leading up to World War 2, and were used to replace the many by now elderly early saloons.

Internally, seating for 40 or 44 was a mixture of transverse and longitudinal. This stock survived until 1981.

All successor rolling stock is still in daily revenue-earning service, and is discussed subsequently.

The second batch of electric locomotives with BTH equipment was much more box-like in shape than the original batch shown on the previous page. This is No 11, photographed at Willesden Green.
Ian Allan Library/Bucknall collection

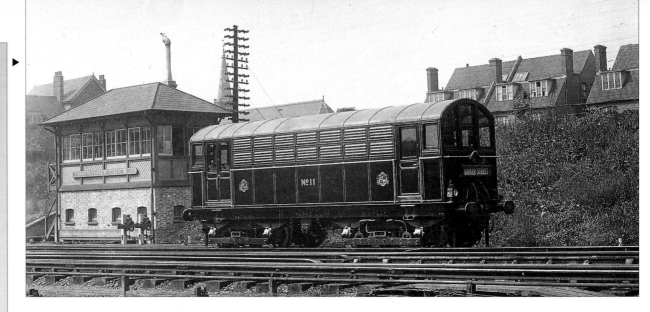

The Beyer Peacock 'A' class 4-4-0Ts which survived electrification of much of the Metropolitan were fitted with cabs and many had their condensing gear removed. Locomotive No 26 is seen in this latter condition, and also sports a later style chimney. No 26 lasted in Metropolitan service from 1868 until 1926, and survived another 22 years at Pelaw Main colliery. *H. Gordon Tidey/Lens of Sutton*

The 'F' class 0-6-2Ts of 1901 all lasted for half a century or more. Metropolitan No 93, later L52, is seen here at around the middle of its life.
Locomotive Publishing Co

The Class G 0-6-4Ts were built, somewhat surprisingly, with express passenger work in mind. These were heavy and powerful locomotives and all were named. This is No 97, *Brill*.
Author's collection

The 4-4-4Ts of Class H were of a graceful and fast design, and extended to eight in total. No 107 is seen here on a Baker Street-bound train on 21 May 1934 at Chalfont & Latimer. *Author's collection*

Class E 0-4-4T No L44, now preserved as Metropolitan No 1, is about to run round its railtour train at Stanmore in October 1961. In the background is a train of 1938 tube stock, complete with a 1927 trailer (far left), which at that time was needed to provide a seven-car formation. *Ian Allan Library*

The interiors of the Q stock were typical of their era, which dated from the 1920s. This is Q23 Driving Motor car No 4248, pictured at the LT Museum where it now resides. *John Glover*

This F stock train is departing from Aldgate as the 17.14 to Uxbridge, while the CO/CP stock train on the right will form the 17.28. The date is 30 May 1962; this area is now completely underground.
L. Sandler

A Great Northern & City line Third Class control trailer car, by now under Metropolitan Railway ownership. This shows the door arrangements and the wooden body construction.
Ian Allan Library

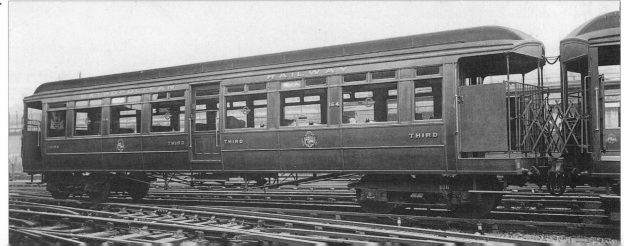

Metropolitan Class H
4-4-4T No 110. The undated
picture includes a lower
quadrant signal, as used by
the company.
Ian Allan Library

0

Ex-GWR pannier tank
No 7739, now L98, cruises
down the 1 in 267 gradient
from Northwood to Pinner
with an engineers' service
on 15 January 1969.
K. P. Lawrence

An electric train, converted from the original 'Ashbury' steam stock, was photographed in 1908 outside the old car shed at Neasden. The livery was cream and teak.
Ian Allan Library/Bucknall collection

A 1921-built Driving Motor car for the Metropolitan Railway. This is car No 117, which included three sets of hand-operated double doors each side. That nearest the luggage compartment is narrower than the rest.
Locomotive Publishing Co

A train of the well-known electric stock of MV (later T) stock is ready to depart from Watford. Leading vehicle is Driving Motor No 207, which was of the batch provided with side buffers, screw couplings and vacuum brakes. Pairs of these DMs were used with five coaches of steam stock to make up seven-car trains.
Ian Allan Library

The ex-GW pannier tank engines never looked totally at home on London Transport metals; this was the second locomotive to be numbered L90, seen at Neasden on 8 November 1969. It is in less than pristine condition, surrounded by the customary detritus of a steam depot. This 0-6-0PT, formerly numbered 7760 and from the North British Locomotive Co build of 1930, spent the decade from 1961 to 1971 in the LT fleet.
Peter Ashton

3. THE LONDON TRANSPORT ERA

The growth of the Metropolitan empire had taken it from its early days during the sulphurous origins of the Underground, to an altogether much larger scale undertaking.

By the 1930s, the Metropolitan could boast a main line which extended over 50 miles from its Baker Street headquarters to Verney Junction in deepest Buckinghamshire, a seven-mile branch from Harrow to Uxbridge, and lesser branches to Watford, Chesham and Brill. Freight and parcels traffic were both encouraged, and facilities provided in many locations. Nearer to London, the City services extended to both Hammersmith and Kensington Addison Road (now Olympia) in the west. The company provided the Circle Line services jointly with the Metropolitan District, as well as those on the East London and the GN&C lines. But was that enough to make the Metropolitan a real main line railway?

The tube railways of the Underground system date from the 1890s, with the major building work in central London taking part in Edwardian times. One quarter of the route network of the tubes, which form the core of today's Underground, was built in this heady era; until the coming of the Victoria Line in 1968-72, there was negligible further construction in what in today's ticket terms is central area Zone 1.

The formation of the Underground Group represented the first major step towards the ultimate goal of complete integration of London's local passenger services. By means of financial control, effected through the agency of a holding company known as the Underground Electric Railways Co of London (UERL), administrative unification had been achieved before World War 1 of the services provided by the Metropolitan District Railway, the deep level tube railways and the London General Omnibus Co. It was mainly after World War 1 that the Underground interests were extended to the privately owned tramways and to bus services in the outer areas. By 1933, some 60% of the passenger journeys in the London area were provided under the direction of the Underground Group.

This group of services thus comprised rail, bus, tram, trolleybus and coach interests. Outside the group, and in competition with it, were the suburban services of the four main line companies, the trams of the London County Council and other municipal owners, about 130 independent bus and coach owners, and the Metropolitan Railway.

In this competitive situation, tube development was effectively inhibited; it was felt that the problem could be resolved only by completing the process of unification upon which the Underground Group had already embarked. It was to achieve this purpose that the London Passenger Transport Board (LPTB) was to be created.

Only one group of undertakings was not proposed for incorporation in the LPTB. This single and important

exception was the group of suburban services of the main line railways (and joint lines) within what became known as the London Transport Area. Roundly, this was within a 25-mile radius from Charing Cross. To the northwest of London, the Area extended to the far side of Amersham.

The main lines carried nearly one-eighth of all passengers — road and rail — for journeys within the London Transport Area. Should the Metropolitan Railway be treated as one of those main line railways, or as part of the Underground? The company itself had decided views. The Metropolitan company recognised:

• that the co-ordination of London passenger transport was a sound objective of official policy;
• that the elimination of wasteful competition was right;
• that traffic regulation to prevent congestion in streets was right;
• that some central authority was needed, to ensure public requirements and convenience should be considered within the economic limits of income imposed by a reasonable scale of fares.

However, the Metropolitan did not accept unified ownership as an objective in itself. In a bid to retain its independent existence, the Metropolitan stated its view that there were other means of achieving the same ends. The preferred method was for itself to be made a member of (what became) the Standing Joint Committee of the LPTB and the main line railway companies. This, besides the co-ordination and development of local services in the Area, was to initiate a revenue pooling scheme. Pooling, the Metropolitan argued, was right in essence, methods and objectives as a means of co-ordination.

As adopted, 'pooling' was a means of dividing traffic receipts, net of working expenses, between two or more companies. This would be computed between any pair of points between which there was competition for traffic; distribution had to be on a mutually agreed basis. It also required an element of common approach to the setting of rates, while the whole needed a bureaucracy in order to sustain it. It might be added that in the first year of operation, the percentages due to each company were expressed to five decimal places. This was in the days

when mechanical calculators were unsophisticated, and computers unheard of!

But Sir Henry Maybury, Chairman of the London & Home Counties Traffic Advisory Committee, would accept none of the Metropolitan's arguments. Speaking in 1931, he asserted that:

The Metropolitan differs in many important aspects from the main line railways. By far the larger part of its traffic is in the inner-ring of London, the traffic on the main line being comparatively unimportant and the system is very much interlocked with the whole of the Underground system of London.

He also felt that it would not be possible for the London Passenger Transport Board (LPTB) to take over the passenger part of the Metropolitan Railway Co's operations without taking over the goods part, another idea which had been floated.

Needless to say, the LPTB, or London Transport for short, came into existence on 1 July 1933. London Transport took over the ownership and operation of the whole of the complex of services described, and thus it incorporated the Metropolitan Railway Co.

There is little doubt that the Metropolitan included a curious range of acquisitions for the fledgling LPTB. In July 1933, the company's rolling stock assets, which

◄◄ Moor Park today has four platforms and the linking footbridge has become a subway. Metrovick Bo-Bo No 11 *George Romney* stands in the old southbound platform in March 1961 with a service for Baker Street. *F. Hornby/Colour-Rail (LT12)*

◄ A train of P stock in ex-works condition, with Driving Motor No 14208 nearest to the camera, stands at Ruislip in May 1961. The service is for Baker Street. Trains were terminating here rather than Uxbridge on this weekend. *J. S. Laker/Colour-Rail (LT147)*

passed to its new owners, consisted of the following:

- 36 steam locomotives
- 21 electric locomotives
- 104 hauled coaching stock
- 211 electric motor cars
- 422 electric trailers, including driving trailers
- 100 service vehicles
- 544 freight vehicles
- 42 horse-drawn goods and parcels road vehicles
- 29 road motor vehicles

In most categories other than electric units, the Metropolitan was the major source of vehicles to the LPTB. Under London Transport, plans were made quickly to disentangle that organisation from what were considered to be the more marginal activities. In the words of the 1935 Annual Report, the distaste is almost palpable:

> The principal efforts (of the LPTB)...have been directed towards bringing the standards and practices of the former Metropolitan Railway, which had been operated on lines more akin to those of a main line company, into conformity (with the UERL).
> It was first necessary to explore the extent to which the detached railways could be welded together into a single system...

The reality was rather less sombre. The major events of the next few years affecting the former Metropolitan were, in chronological order:

1935, 30 November. Withdrawal of all services from Quainton Road to Brill. The justification given was that the daily activities amounted to fewer than 50 passenger journeys being made, and only 20 tons of freight traffic dealt with.

1936, 30 March. Extension of Metropolitan Hammersmith & City services from Whitechapel to Barking.

1936, 4 July. Withdrawal of all passenger services from Aylesbury to Verney Junction. Curiously, this event escaped direct mention altogether in the Annual Report for that year. Freight traffic under LNER auspices survived until 1947.

1937, 1 November. Steam operations for the passenger services north of Rickmansworth, the northern outpost of electrification since 1925, were transferred to the London & North Eastern Railway. From the same date, all freight operations passed to the LNER. The LNER purchased the four 'G' class 0-6-4Ts of 1915, the eight 'H' class 4-4-4Ts of 1921, and the six 'K' class 2-6-4Ts of 1925. Two of each class survived until the end of the LNER in 1947, while their previous duties were assumed by a variety of types. Also included in the sale were 252 goods wagons and 13 brake vans. At the same time, parcels facilities were withdrawn from all the Metropolitan's own stations.

1938, 4 December. New terminus opened at Uxbridge for the Metropolitan Line on the present Uxbridge High Street site.

1939, 11 June. First general fares increase since the inception of the LPTB, with the opportunity taken to equalise fares levels. This affected, particularly, the Stanmore branch, on which the Metropolitan had always charged higher fares since its opening. The net result had been a diversion of traffic by bus to Edgware, Northern Line station. (It may be mentioned here that fares on the Metropolitan main line north of Harrow used to be determined by the LNER/BR rather than the Underground.)

1939, 7 October. Withdrawal of all Pullman Car services.

►
Work is under way at Northwood on the widening works in July 1961. A complication was that the original tracks became the fast lines with their platforms removed, while the new slow lines needed new platforms constructed. In this picture taken looking north, the original tracks are in the foreground.
G. M. Kichenside

►►
Steam haulage north of Amersham was *de rigueur*; after all, it could be argued that the 1960 electrification only moved the boundary post seven miles further north. On 26 May 1963, Class 5 4-6-0 No 45709 leaves Amersham tender first with a train of steam stock.
The late J. P. Mullett/Colour-Rail

1939, 20 November. Extension of the Bakerloo Line from a new junction at Baker Street to Finchley Road with two new stations at St John's Wood and Swiss Cottage, plus resignalling and realignment of tracks northwards to Wembley Park. Provision of flyovers at Neasden for access to the reconstructed depot and for the Stanmore branch at Wembley Park.

Regarding passenger services at Quainton Road, these lingered on under the LNER/BR until the 1960s. On weekdays in 1962, six trains per day were provided in each direction. These local services mostly ran between Aylesbury and Woodford Halse, though the odd one might

extend as far north as Nottingham, or south to London. With a change at Aylesbury, it took a stately 1¼hr or thereabouts for the 44 miles to Marylebone.

For Monday to Friday London commuters, the only relevant services were:

07.03	dep	Quainton Road	arr	18.30	18.50	19.30
07.12	arr	Aylesbury Town	dep	18.20	–	19.20
07.23	dep	Aylesbury Town	arr	18.13	–	19.13
08.22	arr	Marylebone	dep	17.14	17.44	18.14

During the 1930s, Eastcote, Harrow-on-the-Hill, King's Cross (Met), Rayners Lane, Ruislip Manor and Queensbury

Rayners Lane was a 1938 station reconstruction in which the shops were built out to the 'other' side of the pavement, thus ensuring that many non-users of the Underground found themselves almost within the station. As a commentator has noted: 'There is absolutely no chance of a passer-by not noticing this station'. This photograph was taken on 11 April 1998. *John Glover*

A Hammersmith train of CO/CP stock leaves Moorgate on 24 August 1963, with the Barbican redevelopment yet to start. The results of bomb damage are all around. *L. Sandler*

stations were reconstructed, while Aldgate East was rebuilt to free up the Aldgate junctions and thus allow Metropolitan trains to be projected to Barking and Upminster. This also resulted in additional rolling stock orders. At Moorgate, direct interchange was provided between the Metropolitan, the Northern City and the City branch of the Northern Line.

These were the works completed under the 1935-40 New Works Programme, though some stemmed from other commitments. World War 2 resulted in further work being postponed *sine die*; for the Metropolitan Line of London Transport the principal loss was the provision of two additional electrified tracks between Harrow-on-the-Hill and Rickmansworth, and the electrification of the line thence to Amersham and the branch to Chesham. But the postwar world was changing. The financial problems of peak hour operation were nothing new, but the growing

In 1960, the Barbican redevelopment was yet to start; one of the first actions was to realign the four tracks between Barbican and Moorgate. This eliminated the previous curved formation, the start of which is seen here. In this view, an F stock train leaves Moorgate with a Saturday service for Uxbridge, with bomb damage still apparent 15 years after the end of World War 2. *H. Luff/Colour-Rail (LT202)*

On 23 May 1954, a *Railway World* special headed by Metropolitan 'E' class Hawthorn Leslie 0-4-4T locomotive No L48 (formerly Metropolitan Railway No 81) prepares to leave Aylesbury. *Colour-Rail*

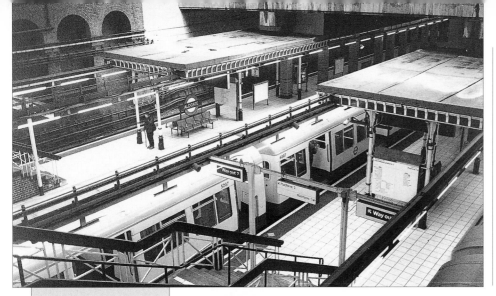

drift of population from the centre of London to the inner and then the outer areas was about to be discouraged by the creation of Green Belt planning controls. No longer could the rail traffic expansion, which the Metropolitan in its earlier days itself had fuelled through its Estates Company, be taken for granted. It was such concerns which led to the final abandonment in 1953 of the partially completed Northern Line extensions beyond Edgware. Edgware itself, though, is a mere 10 miles or so from Charing Cross.

However, the Metropolitan extended far beyond such a radius; what was destined to be the future Underground terminus of Amersham is 25 miles from the centre of the capital, while Aylesbury is 14 miles further still. On the other hand, both are served also by the successors of the Great Central Railway. Would electrification of the Metropolitan ever be justified?

There is never much room in city locations, but Aldgate station seems to have achieved a remarkably spacious arrangement. This view is looking towards Baker Street; the centre platforms are the terminating roads, while the outer ones are used by the Circle Line trains. *John Glover*

The Widened Lines east of King's Cross were photographed on 5 August 1976 from a Moorgate-bound Eastern Region service. A down train, probably empty stock, is approaching behind a Class 31. To the right is the Metropolitan Line, with BR Southern Region-type huts occupying the land in between. *Martin Higginson*

This was the new era of the nationalised transport system. On 1 January 1948 the London Transport Executive and the Railway Executive together assumed the obligation of providing an efficient, adequate, economical and properly integrated system of passenger transport in the LT area.

First moves of the new organisation were not encouraging. The British Transport Commission parent body had created a London Plan Working Party. Reporting in 1949, it gave the Amersham electrification scheme no more than lukewarm support. The argument seemed to be little more than that as the Parliamentary powers were available and the contract drawings had been made, we might as well get on with the job.

The Working Party did, however, discuss rolling stock types, suggesting that outer-suburban stock needed a high seating capacity but with limited boarding and alighting requirements. In the in-town area, though, the need was for a high overload capacity requiring ample standing space. This could only be achieved at the expense of seats, while the doors needed to allow rapid loading and unloading.

They drew attention to London Transport's experimental compromise rolling stock for the proposed Amersham electric services. This work, which gave birth eventually to the A stock of 1960 onwards, was considered unsatisfactory for a number of practical reasons. In the event, the A stock seems likely to achieve a working life of the best part of half a century. Even allowing for the benefits of refurbishment during its life, this hardly suggests that the design adopted had any incurable faults.

In the short term, though, the four-tracking and electrification scheme was not pursued. The rolling stock soldiered on. Alone among London Underground operations, all the main line services except those to Uxbridge were worked by compartment stock. Air-operated doors on these routes? Never!

A new power-signalling box at Rickmansworth was brought into operation in 1953 and work on the layout at Wembley Park to separate conflicting operations was pursued.

◄ The new flyovers west of Barking station were intended to separate the various conflicting train movements. The work was carried out by BR Eastern Region in conjunction with the Tilbury line electrification. This view, of 30 July 1958, was taken from the flyover which was to carry westbound London Transport trains over the main Fenchurch Street to Southend lines. An eastbound train of CO/CP stock for Dagenham is approaching.
Author's collection

Capital expenditure was severely limited. Traffic growth on London Transport services during the interwar years now turned to slow decline, while severe staff shortages compromised service quality. But 1956 brought the news that the Metropolitan scheme was to go ahead, albeit in a slightly reduced form, with the four-tracking ending at Watford South Junction where the Watford branch diverges. In that same year, centralised signalling for the Farringdon to Liverpool Street section was commissioned, with four signalboxes replaced by one. Reconstruction at Notting Hill Gate was also started; this was the largest postwar station reconstruction to date.

Rickmansworth became a point for changing locomotives, thus adding a delay of about 4min to all services proceeding further north. The 1957 timetable shows 56min as a standard time from Baker Street to Amersham. In 1998, the A stock's best time is 43min for the 23.59 miles.

By contrast, the best time from Marylebone in 1957 with no engine changes to worry about and steam traction throughout was also about 56min. It is now 36min by Chiltern Railways. In both comparisons, similar stopping patterns have been used.

For a number of years London Transport had a fleet of steam locomotives for engineering duties. This was increased with the acquisition of ex-GW 0-6-0 pannier tanks, although some of the older Metropolitan locomotives were consequently withdrawn.

Those locomotives which were associated with the Metropolitan and were still in service on 1 July 1960 are described below.

L44/6/8 Originally Metropolitan Class E 0-4-4T locomotives, built at Neasden in 1896 or by Hawthorn Leslie in 1901 (L46). Constructed to haul passenger trains between Rickmansworth and Aylesbury.

L52 Originally Metropolitan Class F 0-6-2T, built by the Yorkshire Engine Co in 1901 for freight duties on the Aylesbury line, but subsequently used for general service, including shunting.

L54 0-6-0ST built by Peckett for the Metropolitan Railway in 1899 for yard work at Finchley Road and Harrow.

L90-L95 Six ex-GWR 0-6-0PTs built 1929/30 for electrification works and other duties; a total of 13 were at one time or another owned by LT before the final withdrawal of steam traction.

The new rolling stock order for the A60 units was let in 1957 to Cravens of Sheffield. Initially, this was for 62 four-car units or 248 cars in total. The order was later expanded by a further 216 cars (54 units) of A62 stock for the Uxbridge services.

The first stage of the electrification scheme was inaugurated on 12 September 1960, when terminating electric trains at Rickmansworth were extended to Amersham and to Chesham. At this stage, Metropolitan-hauled trains were still provided to Aylesbury, and the A stock deliveries had yet to start. Public service for the new trains began in June 1961.

The A stock did not meet with unqualified acclaim. The loss of the compartment stock was a sad blow to many. London Transport defended its position with a mixture of reasons:

- power doors and through gangways for emergency use were by then a requirement for operation in the single-track tunnels between Baker Street and Finchley Road;
- saloon type cars met the mixed requirements for out-of-town and in-town traffic better than compartment stock; and
- the trains had been built to the maximum width the tunnels would take, and a width of 7ft 4in (allowing for an 18in gangway) could either offer 2+2 seats each 21-2in wide, or 3+2 seats each 17.5in wide. LT said 'with five a side, 80 more seats can be given on each train, and 17.5in is not an unreasonably small amount for the average passenger'.

The LTE did give way, though, on the contouring of the seats and the slope of the luggage racks. These were modified, and hooks were added for umbrellas. In retrospect, the whole episode was perhaps more of a comment on the values of the 1960s and the people whom the Metropolitan Railway had enticed to live in Metro-land.

9 September 1961 saw the end of Metropolitan services beyond Amersham and hence steam traction for passenger trains on the Underground. A 'Farewell to Steam' special was run from Baker Street to Amersham and back, while operation beyond to Aylesbury became the exclusive responsibility of British Railways from 11 September.

This left the four-tracking and the Watford branch electrification to be completed, which work was finished on 15 June 1962. New services were inaugurated on 18 June. With a real addition to track capacity, this allowed peak service frequencies to be increased to 20 trains per hour north of Harrow, faster journey times, and a clock-face departure pattern. Interchange with British Railways services was provided at Harrow-on-the-Hill, Chorley Wood, Chalfont & Latimer and Amersham. At Moor Park, interchange was possible between fast and local Metropolitan services at the reconstructed four-platform station. Elsewhere on the new four-track section, platforms were provided only on what became the slow lines to the eastern side of the formation.

The last of the T stock compartment vehicles were withdrawn in October 1962.

The Metropolitan main line now entered a period of stability, the long-sought-for modernisation having now been brought to a successful conclusion.

Elsewhere on the system, the building of new grade-separated junctions at Barking to avoid all conflicting movements between Underground trains and those of British Railways were completed in 1959-60. The work was part of that undertaken under the London, Tilbury and Southend line BR electrification.

In the City, plans were drawn up in 1961 for the implementation of the Corporation's Barbican development. This was to lead to the diversion (on a much straighter

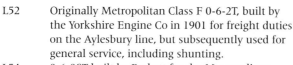

This picture of Euston Road with King's Cross in the background shows the disruption which can be caused by major alterations to a cut-and-cover railway. The occasion was the construction of a new ticket hall for the Metropolitan Line and widening of the concourse. This photograph was taken on 8 November 1939, but work was not completed until 1941. *Modern Transport*

The 17.48 Marylebone to Aylesbury is in the charge of Fowler ex-LMS Class 4 2-6-4T No 42157 as it enters Rickmansworth on 15 June 1962. Both the locomotive and the first coach bear the standard warning of overhead live wires, but there was never an equivalent for the third/fourth rail. *L. Sandler*

Information technology may provide wonders, but a simple message such as which of two platforms the next train to Chesham will leave from needs but a simple sign. This example may be found at Chalfont & Latimer. It was photographed on 6 March 1997. *John Glover*

Uxbridge station, dating from 1938, features stained glass windows which greet arriving passengers as they leave the platform area and wrestle with the automatic ticket gates. These are the only such windows on the Underground, and fit in well with the station's claimed 'cathedral quality'. *John Glover*

◄ Metrovick locomotive No 10 *W. E. Gladstone* approaches Northwood in August 1953 with an Aylesbury to Liverpool Street train. This was then a double-track section of railway.
C. R. L. Coles

◄ The Chesham branch had a visitor around 1952 in the form of this BUT/AEC railbus. It is seen here before departure from Chalfont & Latimer. The three-car unit consisted of two powered cars and a centre trailer, the whole weighing 40.5 tons and seating 110. They were tried on a number of branches, but it is understood that ride quality in these four-wheeled vehicles left much to be desired.
Author's collection

1938 stock trains cross between Canons Park and Stanmore in 1978. The driver of the train on the left has already reversed his marker and tail lights.
John Glover

alignment) of the Metropolitan and the Widened Lines tracks between Aldersgate & Barbican (now plain Barbican) and Moorgate. This major work was not finished until 1966.

Further work at King's Cross (Metropolitan) filled in the former central bay platform, allowing the provision of a larger and much more spacious concourse.

In 1963, a new London Transport Board took control of the Underground, responsible to the Minister rather than the now abolished BTC. There was a new financial regime, and pooling schemes with British Railways were ended.

10 January 1963 saw also the centenary of the Metropolitan Railway and indeed that of the Underground as a whole. A series of commemorative events was held, the most notable of which was perhaps a parade of historic and modern rolling stock at Neasden on 24 May.

The withdrawal of the Underground from that erstwhile Metropolitan company, the Great Northern & City, started in 1964. Opened in 1904, the GN&C was acquired by the Metropolitan in 1913. The GN&C was subsumed into the Northern Line after the formation of the LPTB, in preparation for the part of the 1935-40 New Works Programme of

The 1972 Mk II stock has now all been transferred to the Bakerloo Line, but it is seen here in 1985 at Finchley Road on both northbound (on the left) and southbound services. The approaching train is passing beneath the mercury filled tubes which, should they be broken, are designed to stop any surface stock gauge train from entering a tube-dimensioned tunnel.
John Glover

An A stock train approaches Liverpool Street for Aldgate in July 1990. Beyond the signalbox are the remains of the link between the Metropolitan and the Great Eastern, which diverges to the right and linked into Platform 1 of the main line station.
John Glover

The Widened Lines used to carry trains from the Great Northern. Here, a pair of Cravens Class 105 units breast the steep rise up into Farringdon with a train for Moorgate, while A stock trains cross each other west of the main platforms. The date is 5 August 1976. *John Glover*

1938 stock was the mainstay of the Bakerloo for most of the 40 years until part of it was split off to form the Jubilee Line. A train of 1938 stock is pictured in Neasden in 1983. *John Glover*

Northern Line expansion which, in the end, was never completed. Tube gauge trains took over the Northern City service, as it became known, from 1939.

The section of the GN&C between Finsbury Park and Drayton Park was closed to allow Victoria Line construction to proceed; closure of the whole line to Moorgate was completed a decade later on 3 October 1975. The line was reopened as part of the Great Northern electrification and under British Railways ownership during 1976.

For services on the Hammersmith & City and the Circle Line, tenders were sought in 1967 for 212 cars of what

became the high density C stock. While the new trains for the Metropolitan main line resulted in wholesale scrapping of the displaced trains, the Uxbridge replacements resulted in some cascade of trains elsewhere on the surface lines system. The C stock order was part of a renewal process which was eventually to reduce surface stock on the Underground system to three types only.

London Transport was transferred to the control of the Greater London Council on 1 January 1970, where it remained until 29 June 1984 when the undertaking was renationalised as London Regional Transport. The most

The arrangements at Farringdon after the 1933 reconstruction can be judged from this track diagram. In particular, it shows the link to the Widened Lines west of the station platform, and the link to Blackfriars. All former goods facilities are no longer in existence. *Modern Transport*

The Hammersmith & City Line is worked exclusively by C stock, as seen here in 1983 approaching Ladbroke Grove with a Whitechapel-bound service. *John Glover*

Metro-land was in many ways disarmingly ordinary. Yet, this suburban street has a bus stop situated close to a zebra crossing which in turn leads to...! Dollis Hill station was opened in 1909; it is today a modest station with an island platform. This is reached via a subsurface ticket office, which has entrances north of the line as shown here from Burnley Road and also the southern side. The picture was taken on 28 December 1996.
John Glover

Rayners Lane on Easter Saturday 1998 demonstrates the prowess of the Harrow Fuschia Society in Metro-land. The notice also delivers a stern warning, as it 'kindly requests that passengers refrain from walking on this flower bed'. Presumably it is all right to walk on the rest?
John Glover

memorable episode of this period was the 'Fares Fair' policy of the GLC. This resulted in fares being reduced by an average 32%. The reduction was challenged and eventually overturned in the House of Lords. The five Law Lords ruled on 17 December 1981 that the actions were unlawful under the terms of the 1969 Act through which the GLC had gained control of LT.

While this affected the Metropolitan no more and no less than any other part of the LT operations, the ensuing debate on

- what fares are acceptable?
- what level of service should be provided? and
- what amount of subsidy should be made available and from whom?

dominated thinking for several years. As a response, fares were raised by 96% in March 1982.

The GLC era also saw the end of steam haulage on the Underground; steam had been retained for nearly three years longer than on British Railways. Although used only for engineering trains and other non-passenger duties, and principally though not exclusively on the Metropolitan, the availability of ex-BR Western Region 0-6-0PTs proved to be more economic than the purchase of a new diesel fleet. The last run, from Barbican to Neasden, took place on 6 June 1971.

A preoccupation from the mid-1960s onwards was the growth of commuter traffic on the Metropolitan and its distribution within central London. The building of the Bakerloo extension from Baker Street to Finchley Road was an earlier response to a situation which was putting extreme pressures on the twin tracks of the Metropolitan north of Baker Street. One particular advantage of this scheme was the cross-platform interchange available between the two services at Finchley Road itself, easing journeys to the West End. While the Metropolitan provides excellent City access, the railway's line of route has always studiously avoided West End destinations.

With the forecast of more traffic for dispersal south-wards from Baker Street, the planners decided that the most effective means of increasing capacity was to separate the two Bakerloo branches. The original Elephant & Castle to Queen's Park (and beyond over BR metals) service would become self-contained, with a new depot constructed at Stonebridge Park. The Stanmore branch and its extensions to Baker Street would use its own new platforms at Baker Street and take a new routeing via Bond Street and Green Park to a temporary terminus at Charing Cross. Overrun tunnels took the track a good quarter of a mile further, almost reaching Aldwych. That much was Stage 1, and the whole was opened as the Jubilee Line on 1 May 1979.

The subsequent stages went through any number of alterations. The problems which defeated the planners were the identification of the eventual destination (Thamesmead, Lewisham and Hayes being among those considered) and the relationship of the extension to the East London Line. The final politically inspired answer was the Jubilee Line Extension of 1999, which abandoned the Charing Cross terminus and diverted the Jubilee via Westminster and Waterloo to Docklands and a north-facing terminus at Stratford.

4. THE METROPOLITAN TODAY

Metropolitan Main Line

Rolling Stock

The A stock trains were constructed in two all but identical batches, totalling 464 vehicles. Each vehicle (a Driving Motor DM or Trailer T) offers 54 seats (DMs) or 58 seats (Ts). The DMs have two pairs of double doors and one single door per side for passenger use, and the Ts three pairs of double doors.

Entering service from 1961 onwards, the already venerable A stock has undergone two extensive sets of modifications. First was the conversion for one-person operation between 1985 and 1986. The trains, which originally were completely interchangeable, became specialised in the sense that only 24 four-car sets (later 26) had both cabs converted. This avoided the need for (and cost of) some of the fittings on one end of each of the remaining sets, which were henceforth deemed to be centre vehicles. The

The 1973 stock provides all Piccadilly Line trains, and a refurbished unit is seen here on the eastbound line at Ruislip Manor on 11 April 1998. *John Glover*

double-ended sets are required for working singly on the Chesham branch and on the East London Line.

The second and, to the passenger, more noticeable work was the refurbishment from 1992-8 of all units. The author hesitates to use the phrase 'mid-life refurbishment' as this implies their survival until around 2030, but this essentially is what it was. A complete internal refit and the painting of the outside in LUL corporate livery was the result, plus fitting the correct side door enable equipment (CSDE). This prevents the driver from inadvertently opening the doors on the wrong side relative to the platform.

The Metropolitan main line is today operated in its entirety by a maximum of 43 eight-car trains of A stock, plus one four-car train for the Chesham shuttle. A 'spare' component of the fleet is of course needed for maintenance and other purposes, though this still makes the original orders for the equivalent of 58 eight-car trains appear decidedly on the generous side. Around half the Metropolitan main line fleet is sourced from Neasden, and the rest from sidings at Wembley Park, Uxbridge and Rickmansworth.

One result has been that, even allowing for a small overall fleet reduction due to minor mishaps, six four-car trains are available to run the East London Line services.

Baker Street is cramped, as might be expected in a central London station, but the Metropolitan still managed to equip itself with six platforms in total. Metrovick Bo-Bo No 7 *Edmund Burke* emerges from the tunnel with a terminating train in 1959 with a train of 'Dreadnought' compartment stock.
J. G. Dewing/Colour-Rail (LT6)

Barbican station once had an overall roof spanning the four tracks and platforms of the Widened Lines as well as the Metropolitan itself. This view was taken looking eastwards towards Moorgate on 22 April 1998. The overall roof has long since gone. A Fast Amersham A stock train is approaching, with a C stock train for Plaistow on the left. *John Glover*

Baker Street has changed little at Metropolitan-platform level. This view of 11 April 1998 shows an A stock train for Aldgate arriving in Platform 3, as with the Metrovick-hauled train of nearly 40 years earlier. *John Glover*

Main Line Operations

The length of the Metropolitan line and the number of stations involved has for many years resulted in a pattern of operation which more nearly resembles that of a main line railway. Using the midday Monday to Friday timetable as the example, the services may be described as follows. The description refers to the timetable in force during winter 1997-8.

- **Amersham line:** two trains per hour from Aldgate, fast throughout. These services run nonstop Finchley Road to Harrow-on-the-Hill, then again nonstop to Moor Park. They then call all stations to Amersham, and at Chalfont & Latimer connect into the Chesham shuttle service. Journey time from Baker Street to Amersham 43min, average 33mph. (All times are taken from Baker Street, excluding the 16min running time from Aldgate where applicable, since the stand time at Baker Street varies from 1-5min for pathing reasons.)

  Two trains per hour from Baker Street, nonstop Finchley Road to Harrow-on-the-Hill, then all stations to Amersham. There is no Chesham connection. Journey time, Baker Street to Amersham 50min, average 28mph.

- **Watford line:** two trains per hour from Aldgate, fast Finchley Road to Harrow-on-the-Hill, then all stations to Watford. Journey time Baker Street to Watford 39min, average 28mph.

  Two trains per hour from Baker Street, all stations (that is, excluding Jubilee Line stations West Hampstead to Neasden inclusive) to Watford. Journey time, Baker Street to Watford 43.5min, average 25mph.

- **Uxbridge line:** six trains per hour calling all stations, four originating from Aldgate and two from Baker Street. Journey time Baker Street to Uxbridge 38min, average 26mph.

Overall, this produces a cumulative eight trains per hour (tph) service between Aldgate and Baker Street. These

Peak Operations

At the height of the evening peak, the busiest hour sees the number of trains leaving Baker Street nearly double to 25tph, with 60% of these originating from Aldgate. A frequently used pattern of operation is for trains to a given destination to run in pairs, a fast version followed by a slow version. Thus there is a 17.34 and a 17.36 leaving Baker Street for Amersham, followed by a 17.38 Uxbridge and then a 17.41 and a 17.44 for Watford. The stopping patterns of all of these follow those described above. Immediately behind **these** trains are a 17.46 fast to Uxbridge (which runs nonstop Finchley Road to Harrow-on-the-Hill) and a 17.48 slow service.

An additional peak-only operation is provided by the two trains from Aldgate to Chesham, leaving Aldgate at 16.59 and 17.31 respectively. While these trains are on the branch, the shuttle from Chalfont & Latimer is suspended.

Over the course of a busy hour, there are five services to Amersham, two to Chesham, seven to Watford and 11 to Uxbridge.

The Saturday services follow the off-peak Monday to Friday service closely; without the peak supplementation, they require but 29 eight-car trains and one four-car train in service. On Sundays, the Uxbridge trains reduce to 4tph and the Watford's trains all become slow services to ensure that frequencies at Wembley Park, North Harrow and Preston Road are unchanged. The Amersham trains retain the weekday pattern.

Infrastructure

From Baker Street, with its two terminal platforms and two platforms on its through lines to and from the City, the Metropolitan main line enters a tunnel section which is more or less continuous until Finchley Road. Here the Jubilee Line comes to the surface in between the Metropolitan tracks, and the two island platforms provide the best type of interchange arrangements.

North to Wembley Park the Metropolitan retains its outside position, though it is quickly joined by the Chiltern lines of Railtrack on the south side. Wembley Park has six

The 1996 stock for the Jubilee Line has all longitudinal seating, plus additional space set aside for standing passengers which can also accommodate wheelchairs. As a result, seating capacity is reduced to little more than half that of the A stock, if perch or tip-up seats are excluded.
John Glover

▲ trains are almost evenly spaced, but of course there are Circle and Hammersmith & City services running on the same tracks. North of Baker Street, there are 14tph through to Harrow-on-the-Hill, of which 6tph call only at Wembley Park, Preston Road and Northwick Park. Of the 14tph arriving at Harrow, 6tph run to Uxbridge with service gaps of, successively, 10, 12 and 8min.

For the 8tph which continue on the main line, all except the fast Amershams call at North Harrow, Pinner, Northwood Hills and Northwood, giving these stations 6tph in total. The service gaps are, successively, 10, 4 and 16min.

All trains call at Moor Park (8tph). Watford's 4tph are now almost equally spaced at 16, 14min, and the 4tph for Amersham 18, 12min.

platforms, since the Metropolitan now becomes a four-track railway, though the outside platforms on its fast tracks see little use. Immediately after the station, the Jubilee Line diverges to the north side via a dive-under.

North of Wembley Park, Northwick Park and Preston Road island platforms are served by the Metropolitan slow lines only. These are in the centre of the formation, with the fast lines on the outside. Pairing is now by direction. The Chiltern line stays on the south side; so far there have been no platforms on it.

After the six-platformed Harrow-on-the-Hill which serves all lines, the Uxbridge line leaves by a dive-under. The rest of the layout has flat junctions to cater for the absorption of the Marylebone line and the rearrangement of the four Metropolitan running lines. Northwards from here, they are paired separately, main and local, with the main lines on the south side of the formation. Only the local lines have platforms, apart from Moor Park. Beyond Moor Park at Watford South Junction, the four-tracking comes to an end, with the Watford branch leaving to the north over a flat junction. This proceeds eventually to a four-track but only two-platformed terminus.

The Amersham line continues to Rickmansworth, passing the third side of the triangle of lines which allows trains to run direct from there to Watford. The only other junction is at Chalfont & Latimer, where Chesham branch trains depart from a bay adjacent to the main southbound platform. At Amersham, Metropolitan trains normally use the centre platform (No 2) to discharge passengers, then run forward to the sidings before returning to Platform 1 to depart.

Chiltern Trains use Platform 3 at Amersham before departing for Aylesbury, which has two platforms available for trains approaching from the Amersham direction.

Stations not mentioned specifically have two conventional side platforms, as have all those on the Uxbridge branch other than the three-track, four-platform terminus. Uxbridge trains have to absorb Piccadilly Line services at the flat Rayners Lane Junction.

The operation as a whole is made much easier by the four-tracking work which was carried out north of Harrow,

◄ The C stock trains of 1969 vintage had minimal transverse seating arranged in pairs as shown when new. More recently, each bay has been converted to a longitudinal seating pattern with four seats in each, thus retaining the same total number of seats. *Wareite*

Another type of rolling stock found on the East London for a time was the District's D stock. This is the only location where these trains have run as three-car units. In this September 1985 picture, a train accelerates away southwards from Surrey Docks towards one of the New Cross destinations. *John Glover*

On 27 April 1990, an experimentally painted A stock train has taken the East London Line's New Cross branch. This was before the corporate livery had been finally decided upon. *John Glover*

Metropolitan A stock as built, with 1972 Mk II stock for the Jubilee, make partners at Neasden in 1983. The size difference between surface and tube stock is apparent, and this extends to the height of the vehicle floor above rail level. This causes consequential difficulties with platforms. *John Glover*

now nearly 40 years ago. Even so, some might feel that this is rather generous provision for a maximum peak service from there to Watford South Junction of 14tph. Of these trains, only four can use the main line. The other 10 need to use the local line for platform access to the four intermediate stations of North Harrow to Northwood, inclusive.

However, this ignores the fact that north of Harrow-on-the-Hill this was a joint line of the Metropolitan and the Great Central. Formally, though, the infrastructure is nowadays in the hands of London Underground from Harrow to Mantles Wood, a mile or so beyond the far side of Amersham and well beyond the end of the electrified section. This forms one boundary with Railtrack, the other being just south of Harrow-on-the-Hill platforms.

Chiltern Railways

Thus there is a second operator, Chiltern Railways, which uses the same tracks from Harrow northwards. Chiltern's Class 165/0 Network Turbos run every 30min between Marylebone and Aylesbury via Amersham. These trains do

Baker Street contains many distinctive signs, such as this archway which gives access to Platform 5 or the eastbound Circle and Hammersmith & City. It was photographed on 11 April 1998. *John Glover*

▲

'Steam on the Met' 1992 sees GER Class N7 0-6-2T No 69621 with a Stanmore train at Kingsbury in the evening of 18 May as dusk falls. The usual crowds are noticeably absent. *Martin Higginson*

▶

not stop intermediately between Harrow-on-the-Hill and Rickmansworth, and in the peak direction Rickmansworth is omitted for 2hr (morning) and 3hr (evening). Peak services raise the Chiltern frequency to 4tph.

At weekends, Chiltern provides 2tph to Aylesbury via Amersham on Saturdays, but on Sundays most of the service is cut back to run at an hourly frequency between Aylesbury and Amersham only. There, passengers must transfer to the Metropolitan Line. A handful of these services run to or from Marylebone.

Mention of Chiltern should perhaps be a reminder that Marylebone to Amersham best times are around 35min, considerably faster than LUL. Amersham may be reached in 36min (39mph) and Aylesbury in a standard time of 55min (41mph). The best time to Aylesbury via Amersham is 49min by running nonstop Marylebone to Great Missenden, but the county town also has an hourly service

via High Wycombe. This takes 83min over the GW&GC Joint line from Princes Risborough.

Leaf Fall

The other operating hazard is the autumn leaf fall. The stiff climb into the Chilterns and the toll it took of steam locomotive power is of little consequence nowadays; unfortunately, the leaves are still with us. There are modest climbs further south, but it is from the area where the Watford branch diverges that the gradients begin in earnest. Soon after Rickmansworth, they steepen to 1 in 110 and then to 1 in 105 for six miles, until easing a little short of Amersham. This, one might add, is the highest station on London Underground, at 480ft above sea level. This is punishing stuff, and compares for instance with the ruling 1 in 200 on the Great Northern main line out of King's Cross.

The 1983 stock was built to take over all the Jubilee Line services, albeit that it was not delivered until some time after that line opened in 1979. After a 15-year life there, it is now being withdrawn for prospective use elsewhere on London Underground. This view of 1983 stock entering Finchley Road southbound was taken on 4 July 1989. *John Glover*

On Easter Saturday 1998, Chiltern Turbo unit No 165028 hurries through Moor Park on the southbound main line with the 15.06 Aylesbury-Marylebone. This is the only station on the common section of line where Chiltern trains do not stop but Amersham fast trains do. *John Glover*

Moor Park ticket office is a 1961 construction, which gives access to the platforms via a subway. The approach is functional but unexciting. *John Glover*

1992 saw the centenary of railways in Amersham. Metropolitan No 12 *Sarah Siddons* was on duty and was photographed at that station on 16 May. *Martin Higginson*

Metro-land includes all sorts of surprises for the unwary traveller; does one need a ticket to use the footpath to avoid the risk of incurring a penalty fare? This is Chorleywood on 11 April 1998. *John Glover*

The principal weapon of the infrastructure engineer is Sandite, a paste which is deposited on running rails by a train as a means of improving adhesion. Accelerating away from a station and maintaining the momentum is thus made easier. One of the former A60 trailers has been fitted out as a Sandite vehicle, and is used in season by being incorporated into a standard set of A stock.

However, a substantial problem remains on the downhill gradients, notably from Amersham to Rickmansworth. A train needs to decelerate as it approaches a station, and when running downhill the driver has to apply the brakes. The presence of leaves may make the train skid. The driver may apply the brakes harder, and this can stop the wheels revolving, but it does not control the skidding. What it does do is to wear a 'flat' section on the wheel. This results in a need for expensive wheel reprofiling, and in the meantime an uncomfortable, bumpy ride for passengers. It doesn't do the track any good, either!

Sadly, leaf fall is perennial, and despite tree lopping and selective felling (known nowadays as plant management), the problem remains in the Metropolitan's 'garden'. The adopted solution is to insert an additional 3min into the timetable in season for southbound trains, with the effect that the train can approach stations slower and thus minimise the need to brake. The leaf fall period lasts for 10 weeks, from the beginning of October until mid-December.

Chiltern Railways trains are affected similarly.

Jubilee Line

The 1983 stock train built for the Jubilee was one of the less successful designs which the Underground has seen. Notably, the use of four single-leaf doors per vehicle side (three in driving motor cars), is unique on London tube stock. This feature has been less successful in coping with heavy station crowds, and several peak time station stops are in the 40-45sec category. Off peak, most are 20sec, but some 30sec.

The 1983 stock has been replaced by the 1996 stock. This stock was built in connection with the Jubilee Line Extension, but is taking over the whole of the Jubilee Line operation. The 59 trains of 1996 stock, each train formed of two three-car units, are to be maintained at the new Stratford Market depot, but trains will be stabled overnight at Neasden and at Stanmore.

From spring 1998, the off-peak Monday to Friday service has 16tph leaving Charing Cross, of which 8tph work through to Stanmore. The others terminate at Willesden Green (4tph) or Wembley Park (4tph). This results in a rather uneven frequency between the last two points, but the maximum service gap is no more than 7.5min.

At peaks, the service frequency rises to a maximum of 20tph, dropping to 10tph north of Wembley Park. At weekends, the Willesden Green turnback is not used.

A total of 24 trains is required for the present maximum service between Stanmore and Charing Cross on Mondays to Fridays, reducing to 18 on Saturdays and 15 on Sundays.

North of Finchley Road, the Jubilee Line serves the island platforms to Neasden, and at Wembley Park occupies the other side of the island from the Metropolitan services which stop here. Turnbacks are available at West Hampstead, Willesden Green and Wembley Park.

Northwards to Stanmore, the side platforms take over until the terminus, which is again an island. The terminal building, like that at Watford, was built above and clear of the tracks, so that the line could be extended subsequently. Neither has been extended, or indeed seems likely ever to go any further.

Hillingdon station was rebuilt on a new site at the expense of the Department of Transport to facilitate the construction of a diversion for the A40(M). The new station, replacing what has been described as 'the old extended halt', opened on 6 December 1992. This 1997 view looks west towards Uxbridge and an A stock train is approaching. *John Glover*

The centenary of the Chesham branch was celebrated with some limited steam locomotive operations on passenger services, and similar events have continued in most recent years. *John Glover*

The 1996 Jubilee Line stock operates that line's services, and 59 six-car trains have been constructed to provide the services on the extension to Stratford as well. DM No 96066 leads a Stanmore train into Kingsbury on 11 April 1998. *John Glover*

Clearly, the main interest in the Jubilee Line at present is at its eastern end, which is remote from all Metropolitan interest. The opening in 1999 will however have substantial repercussions on the whole of the line's operation and on the rolling stock deployed.

East London Line

The line uses a maximum of six single-ended A stock four-car units, four of which are stabled at New Cross depot. The remaining two run empty from Neasden and return there at night.

Trains run on the double track from Whitechapel south to Surrey Quays. All stations have side platforms only, and between Wapping and Rotherhithe pass through the Brunel tunnel beneath the Thames. These stations are completely underground. The train emerges into full daylight as it approaches Surrey Quays and then proceeds to Canal Junction, where services run alternately to New Cross or New Cross Gate. Both are single platforms in the Railtrack station concerned: New Cross Gate on the Brighton line and New Cross on the South Eastern. The rolling stock depot is on the New Cross (more easterly) branch.

Trains return in the same order as they set out. Both branches are virtually identical in length, but trains on the New Cross leg may need to include a stop at the depot staff platform.

The northbound destination may be Whitechapel or Shoreditch. If the former, trains arrive and depart again from the more westerly Platform 5. Otherwise, they continue to Shoreditch through a deep walled cutting, again to a single-track stub platform. This is a little short of the Great Eastern main line, with which it once made a connection. Trains southwards from Shoreditch use Platform 6 at Whitechapel.

Running times are 12.5min between Shoreditch and New Cross Gate for the 3.67 miles and six intermediate stations (18mph). An allowance for Canada Water is included, though the opening of this new station is intended to coincide with the Jubilee Line Extension. The service described is that on reopening of the line in spring

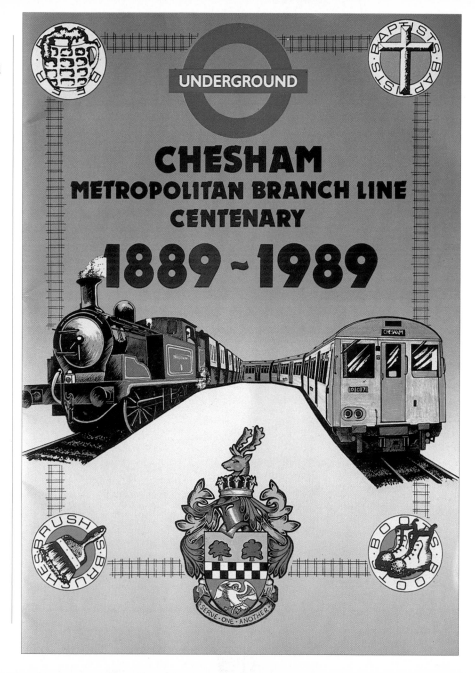

1998 assuming Shoreditch to be operational, after a very prolonged three-year engineering occupation.

Trains reach the rest of the system via St Mary's Curve, from Shadwell towards Aldgate East.

Hammersmith & City and Circle

C Stock

The rolling stock for these services is provided exclusively by the C stock trains. These high-capacity vehicles form six-car trains made up of three two-car sets. The first of the batch of 212 cars (the C69 stock) entered service in 1970. Designed to shift large numbers of short-distance passengers at peak times, they were equipped with four pairs of double doors per side, in a modest saloon length of a mere 49ft 0in. Thirty-two passenger seats were provided in each car with a transverse layout between the sets of doors, and longitudinally in the end sections. There was a follow up order of what became the similar C77 stock; this was for the District Line Edgware Road-Wimbledon service.

One-person-operation was introduced on these two lines in 1984, although minimal work was required on these trains which were introduced with the concept in mind. As with the A stock, mid-life refurbishment was carried out. All seats were converted to a longitudinal layout without the loss of any seats, though the seat width was a mere 17½in after the work was completed, just like the A stock! There were other extensive internal changes,

Drayton Park sees No 313042 arriving with a Moorgate to Finsbury Park only train at the end of the morning peak, while passengers leave an up train. The tunnel section starts immediately at the end of the platform and its large diameter is to accommodate a crossover between the tracks in the tunnel mouth. The date is 6 April 1998. *John Glover*

Chiltern Turbo No 165023 leaves Great Missenden with the 16.36 Aylesbury to Marylebone on 11 April 1998. There is a well-used car park. The down platform is also remarkably wide for what is today no more than a wayside station. *John Glover*

and on the technical side the result was new bogies and new suspension. The work was undertaken between 1990 and 1994.

These units too were outshopped in LUL corporate livery.

A maximum number of 31 trains are required actually in operation to maintain the service on these lines (17 on the Hammersmith & City and 14 on the Circle), but a spare is kept available for use in Edgware Road sidings. Hammersmith is the main depot, but stabling at Barking, Edgware Road and Farringdon is also used.

Hammersmith & City Operations

The basic interval between trains is 8min, as on the Circle with which the H&C trains must dovetail. This requires 14 trains. Service intervals are extended to 10min during the evenings on Mondays to Fridays, and at both ends of the day at weekends.

Hammersmith is the western terminus for all trains, but in the east half the trains terminate at Whitechapel and the rest at Barking. An exception to this is during the evening peak, when Plaistow substitutes for Whitechapel as the turnround point.

An Aldgate-bound train of A stock approaches Neasden at speed on 28 December 1996. In just over a year, the remainder of this fleet of trains will have been refurbished. *John Glover*

Northwick Park station sees an Uxbridge train of A stock arrive on 11 April 1998. Here the Underground lines are grouped northbound fast, northbound local (on which this train is running), southbound local, southbound fast. This changes beyond Harrow. *John Glover*

The station at North Harrow is of simple construction, consisting of two side platforms with steps down to a ticket office and a street exit. An A stock train on the southbound local line approaches on 11 April 1998. The near platform is the northbound local, and almost out of sight to the left are the southbound main and the northbound main lines. *John Glover*

The station car park at Moor Park, as elsewhere on the Underground, is now operated by Meteor Parking. This has implications for LUL staff cars, as the notice makes clear. *John Glover*

Circle Operations

Seven trains in each direction form the Circle service, making a round trip in about 56min and calling at 27 stations. This is an average speed of 14mph. The difficulty with the Circle is its interaction with so many other services coupled with a lack of its own track. Thus the only stretches of line to which it might claim exclusive use are the through platforms (Nos 1 and 4) at Aldgate, Gloucester Road westbound Platform 2 and the curve on both lines between Gloucester Road and South Kensington stations. There is also some flexibility in the two-island platforms available at Edgware Road, though this depends also on their occupation by District Line trains. Apart from that, the choice is a few terminal platforms or sidings, or taking the train somewhere else altogether, such as Whitechapel.

This example is quoted at length, if only to illustrate how difficult it is to regulate such a service if (or, to be realistic, when) something goes wrong. Stand time at terminals is a valuable commodity; the Circle has to do without it. Leaf fall problems are the least of Circle Line worries, but the difficulties of inserting an extra 3min into running times over part of the route for a few weeks of the year hardly bear thinking about.

Infrastructure

The Hammersmith & City Line starts at the three platform faces. The depot is beyond the end of the platforms on the eastern side of the line. H&C trains then negotiate two miles of route on viaduct where the line has side platforms at all the stations. Side platforms are the norm throughout. The H&C then reaches the Great Western main line. It descends to cross this in a subway, rising to run alongside through Royal Oak and to Platforms 15 and 16 at Paddington main line. Entering the cut-and-cover tunnel, it joins the Circle Line at Praed Street Junction.

Circle services joined the original outpost of the Metropolitan at South Kensington, now just one island platform. Outer rail services take their own platform at Gloucester Road, then all swing north to High Street Kensington and its further junctions, and on towards Paddington.

The Circle and H&C enter Edgware Road together, and from here to beyond King's Cross the line is almost wholly underground.

Baker Street Platforms 5 and 6 have been refurbished in a recreation of the original 1863 style. This is where the Metropolitan main line trains to the City join.

Through Farringdon and on to Barbican the Widened Lines can be seen alongside, but Moorgate platforms are now buried below commercial developments. Liverpool Street still retains much of its earlier character, and then Aldgate Junction signifies the divergence of the Circle. This shares the route of the District over the section built jointly by the companies to the recently rebuilt Mansion House.

H&C trains continue to Aldgate East where the District

Line is joined in a trailing junction. There is a short open-air section through Whitechapel, which has two islands and thus is a suitable location for terminating trains.

The line goes underground again to Mile End, where cross-platform interchange with the Central Line is available. It reaches the surface at Bromley-by-Bow and uses the track formerly part of the LT&S line which it now parallels. Plaistow has a turnback platform on the eastbound side.

Approaching Barking, a flyover ensures that cross-platform interchange with LT&S trains is available in both directions. There are stabling sidings beyond the station, although H&C trains can reverse in the station itself when using Platform 3. District Line services continue only to Upminster.

Great Northern Suburban

Today's Moorgate trains are formed exclusively with the dual-voltage Class 313 units, which change from overhead to third rail collection at the changeover point at Drayton Park. The tunnels thence to Moorgate may be the largest diameter bored tube tunnels around, but they are not sufficient for 25kV ac overhead.

All trains descend from Finsbury Park main line station, the former tube section between Finsbury Park and Drayton Park having been annexed for Victoria Line construction and used in part from as long ago as 1964. Trains may return to the main line by use of a crossover at Drayton Park, but after this point there are no junctions on the double track before the terminus at Moorgate. Here, a scissors crossing gives access to both platforms.

A 12tph service is the maximum which is currently provided. There are no services after mid-evening, nor at any time at weekends.

All stations have interchange with other lines, apart from Essex Road and Drayton Park. At Highbury & Islington, there is the only example of cross-platform interchange. This is with the Victoria Line.

5. PLANS FOR THE FUTURE

Of the new schemes which might one day be implemented, CrossRail would have a profound effect on the Metropolitan main line. Conceived as a means of linking rail routes east and west of the central area using a new large gauge tunnel to connect them, a CrossRail scheme would:

- eliminate interchange for many passengers who presently transfer to the Underground or to buses;
- provide faster end-to-end journeys for these passengers;
- achieve greater productivity from the staff and rolling stock operating these services, by reducing the number of turnrounds; and
- add to capacity with new links across the centre, where the most serious problems exist.

The proposed CrossRail scheme would provide an east-west service through a new tunnelled link between Liverpool Street and Paddington, over which 24 trains per hour could be operated. Intermediate stations would be at Farringdon (for Thameslink 2000 and the Metropolitan), Tottenham Court Road (for the Northern, Central and perhaps the Chelsea-Hackney Line), and Bond Street (for the Central and Jubilee Lines).

At the eastern end, CrossRail trains would replace all existing Great Eastern inner suburban services between Liverpool Street and Shenfield via Stratford.

At the western end, CrossRail would replace Chiltern Line services between Aylesbury and Marylebone via Amersham and also the Metropolitan main line services to

Shadwell station is built partly in cut without cover, but the incidence of objects being thrown onto the track has resulted in the provision of this protective covering. An A stock train arrives from Whitechapel bound for New Cross Gate on 18 April 1998, shortly following the reopening of the line after an extended closure. *John Glover*

Chorleywood station (no hyphen since 1965) was built in 1889 and is typical of the Metropolitan's wayside stations of that period. The 16.06 Aylesbury to Marylebone is coasting to a stand on 11 April 1998, but patronage could euphemistically be called 'light'. *John Glover*

The bridge over the Grand Union Canal a little to the south of Watford Metropolitan station sees a southbound departure on 18 April 1998. In the distance is Cassio Bridge Lock, which canal users must negotiate on their way to Birmingham. But this is only one of the 166 locks on the 137 miles of the Grand Union. *John Glover*

The 08.57 from Marylebone arrives at Aylesbury on 11 April 1998 formed of Chiltern Turbo No 165031. This is one of the three-car versions of these units; as all vehicles are powered, this does not affect operational performance.
John Glover

Amersham and Chesham. Access to Paddington would be via a remodelled Neasden South Junction and the present freight-only route towards Acton Wells, then via a new connection to the Great Western main line. The capacity released on the Metropolitan Line could be utilised by enhancing services on the Uxbridge and Watford lines, since the Metropolitan would no longer run to Rickmansworth or points north.

In the west, CrossRail would also replace most of the existing Thames Trains services into Paddington from Ealing Broadway, Slough and Reading. CrossRail is also planned to serve Heathrow, subject to agreement with BAA and Railtrack on access arrangements.

While the project remains formally safeguarded, there seems to be little likelihood of it progressing in the short term. Legal powers also have yet to be acquired. However, other service patterns are possible while retaining the basic concept. London Transport Planning's view is that CrossRail would provide widespread congestion relief and eliminate crowding over most parts of the Underground network.

On the Metropolitan section, the question of power supplies arises. While the Great Eastern and now part of the Great Western are equipped with 25kV ac electrification, and the new central area tunnel could be thus equipped, the Aylesbury link is a mixture of non-electrified and fourth rail dc operation. In route miles terms, it is only four miles or so from Neasden to Harrow-on-the-Hill. Beyond this point, there is no obvious reason why the Metropolitan should not be confined to the slow lines for the journey thence to Watford. The additional four stops from Harrow-on-the-Hill to Moor Park, if made, consume about 5min extra running time.

A 25kV CrossRail operation throughout to Aylesbury seems the most likely outcome. Whether the A stock will have to last until a decision is made and implemented, and new stock constructed, is another matter!

Also in the list of possibilities is the Croxley link. This is a proposal to extend the Metropolitan Line train service via Croxley to Watford Junction.

From the Watford branch, the route would be via a new park-and-ride station at Ascot Road. The route would then proceed via the effectively defunct Railtrack Croxley Green single-track branch and Watford West station. Joining the existing dc lines once occupied by the Bakerloo but nowadays the preserve only of Silverlink's Class 313 units, Metropolitan trains would proceed to Watford High Street and Watford Junction. The present Watford (Metropolitan) station would close.

This would be achieved by the construction of a new 500m viaduct to bridge the A412 road, the River Gade and the Grand Union Canal. The cost of the scheme, which would include doubling the Railtrack branch, is put at £25 million.

Existing Underground users from Harrow and Pinner would gain access to more useful destinations than the present 1925 Watford Metropolitan terminus, for which the problems of a route through Cassiobury Park to the town centre proved insurmountable. Besides giving access to Virgin Trains and Silverlink Services at Watford Junction, Watford is a regional commercial centre and High Street station is well situated. Watford itself also

The East London Line has been extensively modernised by London Underground, besides the rehabilitation of the Brunel tunnels beneath the Thames. A northbound A stock train for Whitechapel is arriving at Wapping on 18 April 1998. *John Glover*

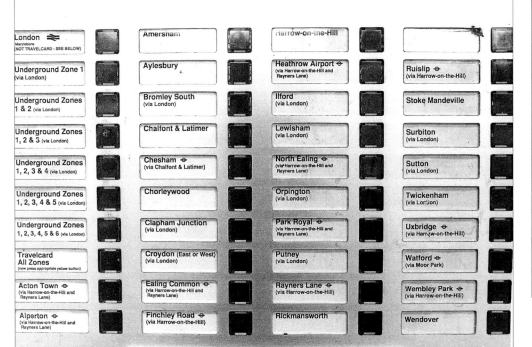

Select your destination

London ⊖ Marylebone (NOT TRAVELCARD - SEE BELOW)	Amersham	Harrow-on-the-Hill	
Underground Zone 1 (via London)	Aylesbury	Heathrow Airport ⊖ (via Harrow-on-the-Hill and Rayners Lane)	Ruislip ⊖ (via Harrow-on-the-Hill)
Underground Zones 1 & 2 (via London)	Bromley South (via London)	Ilford (via London)	Stoke Mandeville
Underground Zones 1, 2 & 3 (via London)	Chalfont & Latimer	Lewisham (via London)	Surbiton (via London)
Underground Zones 1, 2, 3 & 4 (via London)	Chesham ⊖ (via Chalfont & Latimer)	North Ealing ⊖ (via Harrow-on-the-Hill and Rayners Lane)	Sutton (via London)
Underground Zones 1, 2, 3, 4 & 5 (via London)	Chorleywood	Orpington (via London)	Twickenham (via London)
Underground Zones 1, 2, 3, 4, 5 & 6 (via London)	Clapham Junction (via London)	Park Royal ⊖ (via Harrow-on-the-Hill and Rayners Lane)	Uxbridge ⊖ (via Harrow-on-the-Hill)
Travelcard All Zones (now press appropriate yellow button)	Croydon (East or West) (via London)	Putney (via London)	Watford ⊖ (via Moor Park)
Acton Town ⊖ (via Harrow-on-the-Hill and Rayners Lane)	Ealing Common ⊖ (via Harrow-on-the-Hill and Rayners Lane)	Rayners Lane ⊖ (via Harrow-on-the-Hill)	Wembley Park ⊖ (via Harrow-on-the-Hill)
Alperton ⊖ (via Harrow-on-the-Hill and Rayners Lane)	Finchley Road ⊖ (via Harrow-on-the-Hill)	Rickmansworth	Wendover

At Great Missenden, the usual self-service ticket machine carries a remarkable series of destinations, much wider than usual. Who in Great Missenden, one wonders, wants to buy a ticket to Surbiton or to Orpington, in such numbers as to make provision worthwhile? Routeing is also of note; there is a ticket to Heathrow, but one must travel via Rayners Lane and keep out of fare zones 1 and 2 as a result. *John Glover*

regains access to the Underground network.

London Underground needs to submit a Transport &
Works Act application for powers to build the link.
And then there is the East London Line. A few years ago,
London Underground saw this line as having a somewhat
ambiguous status as a separate but not altogether
autonomous part of the Metropolitan Line. In many ways,
it was the poor relation of the Underground, tucked away
in a declining and unglamorous part of London. Times
change, and the line experienced enormous traffic growth
during the 1980s, due largely to regeneration and economic
growth in Docklands. The main line railway, in the form of
Railtrack, is taking an active interest. Line extensions are
possible, and a northern link from Whitechapel to Dalston
along the old North London Line formation to Broad Street
was given Government approval at the beginning of 1997.
However, there was no public funding forthcoming. A
southern extension to join the present Railtrack lines at
Peckham Rye is feasible, while the present stub which ends
at New Cross or New Cross Gate could be turned into
junctions.

In the north, Dalston could be an intermediate terminus
before continuing over the North London Line to Highbury
& Islington.

Many further extensions are possible, all of which
require some capital funding. There are also tricky
calculations to be done concerning line capacity, its
availability, and the priorities for each operator who may
wish to use it.

However, the East London future looks more likely to be
part of the main line railway system again, rather than the
Underground. Or are we likely to see Underground trains
extended over the network now owned by Railtrack, to
places such as Clapham Junction (by routes either north
or south of the river), Croydon or Enfield...? Perhaps the
large fleet of Metropolitan A stock might find long-term
alternative uses, more than justifying that mid-life
refurbishment.

Finally, another railway on the Metropolitan sidelines
was the Great Northern & City. Operated since 1976 as the
principal London end of the West Anglia Great Northern

Railway's (WAGN) inner suburban operation from Welwyn Garden City and Hertford North, its services are billed to stay much the same if and when Thameslink 2000 is implemented. The remaining WAGN outer services will either remain in King's Cross, or share the additional line capacity with the existing Thameslink services. All these will operate over the Widened Lines to Blackfriars and on to southern metals. They are expected to serve a variety of new destinations ranging from Dartford and Ashford International in the east, to Guildford and Horsham in the west. The T2000 scheme will also entail the closure of the Widened Lines section east of Farringdon to Moorgate.

Legal powers for this scheme have yet to be obtained.

Major proposals such as those discussed above all affect the former Metropolitan Railway's interests in one way or another, albeit now as part of a wider network. Such schemes are all very well, but they do not address the basic problems of infrastructure maintenance and looking after what we have. London needs a well presented and well looked after system. The attributes of such a railway were discussed by London Transport in a booklet *Making Vision into Reality*:

'A Decently Modern Metro means:
- New or refurbished trains on all lines.
- More frequent services, faster journeys and less crowding.
- High quality stations providing greater capacity and better standards of service.
- Reliable lifts and escalators.
- New travel opportunities.
- Rebuilt track and restored embankments, tunnels, drainage, etc.
- Better information for customers.
- A safe, secure environment for customers and employees.'

Today's users of the Metropolitan Railway's bequest to London Transport, as subsequently updated, are perhaps the best judges of how well the Metropolitan lives up to these standards.

6. CONCLUSION

▶▶ To many, the Metropolitan Railway was an enigma. Was it just the oldest part of London Underground, or was it really a main line railway without a 'proper' London terminus?

The truth would appear to be somewhere in between. A parallel might be drawn with the former passenger rail businesses of the British Railways Board. Some undoubtedly fitted the InterCity cachet. Others consisted primarily of local services. But there were always the somewhat indeterminate ones. How was it that a service from Bournemouth to London was classified as a Network SouthEast operation, and Gatwick Airport to London as InterCity?

So often the answer is related to history, and nowhere more so than with the Metropolitan. First, it had all the problems of a pioneer in the perseverance the company needed to build its initial line from Paddington to Farringdon. But the difficulties were overcome successfully, and the company went on to become a sizeable force in urban transport. Much of this was due to Pearson, the City solicitor who would not take no for an answer, while Fowler's choice of traction and rolling stock made sure

▶▶ that the whole thing worked.

Secondly, the single-mindedness of Watkin in pursuing an expansionist policy, albeit as much for his own reasons as those of the company, took the Metropolitan far from its urban base. To say that it petered out in the middle of nowhere at Verney Junction, is a little unkind. But this was not in any sense an area from which traffic growth could be expected; in distance terms, Verney is almost identical to that of Brighton from London, and the difference is plain to see.

The Metropolitan was successful in forging worthwhile commercial deals with other railways, and the link with the Great Central was of benefit to both. It was also those links which enabled the company to profit from freight traffics, and these affected especially the Widened Lines connections south of the Thames.

That there are nowadays no passenger railways north of Aylesbury effectively restores the Metropolitan to a truly suburban operation. Today it is without the frills of parcels or other traffics. For 70 years the company enjoyed an independent status; for the last 65 years since 1933 it has enjoyed the benefits and frustrations of being a not entirely homogenous part of a much larger grouping.

The company management in the form of Selbie, the General Manager, saw the then largely open countryside in its hinterland as a major opportunity, and tailored the management strategy accordingly. The use and extension of the powers which the company then had to exploit land holdings for housing purposes was of lasting benefit to its revenues, and Metro-land remains the principal justification for the railway to this day.

This was perhaps an indication of how well the company studied its market. The desire to provide service quality which met the needs of the mobile and well-to-do middle class, whom the Metropolitan itself encouraged to live in the area which it served, was evident. If people were able and willing to pay for First Class comfort, the Metropolitan was happy to oblige, provided it was also profitable for the company. There were also pains taken to provide rolling stock of better than the average standards of the time.

The London Transport era brought a degree of co-ordination which would never otherwise have been achieved. It seems unlikely that the Bakerloo would ever have been allowed to duplicate the Metropolitan's main line to Wembley Park and annexe the branch to Stanmore, under the previous management. The risks would have been too great. Whether the Amersham electrification would (or should) have taken place any quicker is probably unanswerable in retrospect, given the intervention of the war.

Today, London Underground runs a creditable service, which is superior in timings and frequency to that offered in earlier days. The age of the A stock has been disguised, to the extent that it gives a bright and modern appearance. Future challenges revolve around:

- further development of the market;
- upgrading the condition of the infrastructure;
- the CrossRail scheme in whatever form (if any) it might take in future;
- the future of the Croxley link; and
- the competitive position with other operators, principally Chiltern Railways.

The whole is affected by the future form of organisation of London Underground itself and the public sector control which is deemed relevant for the Metropolitan. There are 15 route miles of Metropolitan track outside Greater London, which is doubled if Amersham to Aylesbury is added back on. The parts of the line within London could perhaps stand on their own, but those within Buckinghamshire and Hertfordshire cannot.

However, what the Metropolitan Railway did seem to attract was a degree of affection amongst its customers. Goodwill is a valuable asset for any business, worth real money. Are we as clever today in the transport businesses as we might be in this crucial area?

The title of this book refers to the glory days of the Metropolitan. Glory may be defined as 'fame and honour, won by great deeds'. Which deeds were they? Deeds also have to be executed by people, and most require a supportive economic, social and organisational background. The principal deeds would seem to have been:

- getting the enterprise under way in the first place, culminating in the initial opening in 1863;
- the expansionist days of the later Victorian era;
- the 1920s when continuous improvements were being pursued; and
- the 1960s after the Amersham electrification benefits started to come through.

Or are the real Glory Days yet to come? Readers must make that judgement for themselves.

The old order is displayed with a varnished coach and Metrovick locomotive No 5 *John Hampden* at the LT Museum. *John Glover*

GWR 0-6-0PT No 7715, later L99, was built by Kerr, Stuart & Co in 1930. It was the last of the line to enter London Transport stock in 1963, where it remained until 1970. Today it may be found at the Buckinghamshire Railway Centre at Quainton Road; it was about to take up duty when photographed here on 13 April 1998. *John Glover*

An Aldgate-Watford train of A stock rounds the curve into Farringdon on 22 April 1998. There are three stabling sidings to the right of the train, and a catenary support for the Widened Lines can just be seen as the latter enters a tunnel. *John Glover*

BIBLIOGRAPHY

London's Metropolitan Railway by Alan A. Jackson and published by David & Charles in 1986, ISBN 0 7153 8839 8. This is undoubtedly the major work on the history of the Metropolitan, recounted in great detail. For those who are looking for a more concise volume, there is *The Metropolitan Railway* by C. Baker from Oakwood Press, 1951, reprinted 1960, or *The Metropolitan Line, A Brief History* by Charles E. Lee and published by London Transport in 1972. For a specialised look at the stations, try *London's Underground Stations* by Laurence Menear, Midas Books 1983, ISBN 0 85936 124 1.

On the rolling stock front, there is *Steam to Silver — A History of London Transport Surface Stock* by J. Graeme Bruce and published by Capital Transport, 1983, ISBN 0 904711 45 5. Also, *Steam on the Underground* by Martin Smith, Ian Allan Publishing, 1994, ISBN 0 7110 2282 8. Another title is *The Last Drop: London Transport Steam 1863-1971*, produced by London Transport in 1971.

Other useful sources include *Railway Track Diagrams 5, England South and London Underground* published by Quail Map Company, 1994, ISBN 1 898319 07 3, *London Transport Annual Report and Accounts, Modern Railways* magazine published by Ian Allan, and various timetables, both public and working editions.

ACKNOWLEDGEMENTS

I am grateful to Ron White of Colour-Rail for the provision of some of the illustrations, without which the book would have been that much poorer, and to Mr C. M. Pritchard of PECO who readily agreed to the inclusion of some splendid drawings of Metropolitan locomotives by Ian Beattie, which had appeared previously in the *Railway Modeller*.

Also, of course, thanks to my other picture contributors, including those whose work was extracted from the files of my publishers, and to Ian Allan Publishing themselves from whom the idea for the project stemmed.

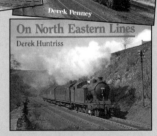